THE HIAWATHA ANTHOLOGY

Stories from Upper Michigan's Pioneer Past
By: Larry Peterson

THE HIAWATHA ANTHOLOGY

Stories from Upper Michigan's Pioneer Past

By: Larry Peterson

Layout and Cover Design:
Stacey Willey, Globe Printing, Ishpeming MI

Copyright © 2020 Larry Peterson

ISBN: 978-0-578-70583-5
Library of Congress Control Number: 0578705834

All Rights Reserved. No part of this book may be used or reproduced in any manner whatsoever without the expressed written permission of the author.

Cover Photo - William and Ina Mae Kefauver appeared in numerous amateur theater productions at the Star Opera House in Manistique during the late 1890s and early 1900s. Photo courtesy SCHS.

You may contact Larry at larryandrebeccapet@yahoo.com.
Additional copies also available at Amazon.com

Dedicated to my parents,
Lawrence and Martha Peterson
who inspired me with a love of history.

Table of Content

1. A Strange Tale of Two Editors 1
2. Captain Bundy and his Gospel Ships. 16
3. The Legend of the Christmas Tree Ship 25
4. The Lumberman's Daughter 38
5. The Downfall of a Dive Keeper 47
6. Pond v. The People 57
7. Utopia in the Northwoods 65
8. Portrait of an Altar Artist 76
9. The Pioneer Life of Elizabeth Allen 85
10. The Last Log Drive 91
11. The Jamestown Lumbering Settlement 97
12. The Voyage of the Griffin 103
13. Charles Ekberg, Pioneer Cobbler. 111
14. The Circuit Rider 116
15. A Lightkeeper's Story 121
16. Alexander Richards and the Flat Iron Block . . . 126
17. John Ira Bellaire, Merchant, Conservationist and Historian 129
18. The McCanna Brothers – Pioneer Lawmen. . . 133

Introduction

I have always delighted in learning about the past. Some of my fondest childhood memories include listening to my aunts and uncles pass on colorful anecdotes told to them by their grandfather, William Caffey, a Civil War veteran from Pennsylvania. History and my great grandfather came alive for me in those stories. It is my hope that the episodes presented here will awaken that same spirit of wonder concerning the rich history that central upper Michigan has to offer. The Hiawatha Anthology is a collection of true stories about some of the people who lived here not so very long ago.

During the early 1860s, the settlement then known as Epsport, on the northern shore of Lake Michigan, was in its infancy. Its few crude dwelling places stood at the mouth of the Monistique River. Arthur J. Spinney and David Boyd operated a steam saw mill near the riverbank. The little hamlet was surrounded by a vast virgin forest of hardwood and pine, interspersed with inland lakes, rivers, streams and cedar swamps. A Chippewa Indian village was located nearby on the shore of one of those inland lakes.

The tiny settlement's population remained stable at about 200 persons though the late 1870s. In 1868, Spinney and Boyd sold the mill to a group of Chicago investors who formed the Chicago Lumbering Company. These investors then resold the company in 1873 to some New York lumbermen led by Abijah Weston. They retained the name of the company but tore down the old mill and replaced it with a much larger, more modern facility. Manistique's days as a lumbering boom town had begun.

The Hiawatha Anthology tells the stories of some of the pioneering men and women who were drawn to Manistique and the surrounding area. They include professionals, sailors, fishermen, lumbermen, farmers, an artist, evangelist, saloon owner and an entertainer. Some migrated here from other parts of the country. Some were immigrants from Scandinavia, Europe and Canada.

Wright E. Clarke arrived in Manistique in April of 1880 and immediately began the publication of the county's first newspaper, The *Schoolcraft County Pioneer*. The charismatic Clarke quickly gained the reputation of a man of integrity, being elected to the village counsel and the Probate judgeship. Clarke was soon joined in Manistique by a young newspaper man from Indiana; Will F. Montgomery who would later establish a competing newspaper, the *Sunday Sun*. "A Strange Tale of Two Editors" tells the story of the intense newspaper rivalry between Clarke and Montgomery, and the scandalous secret the two men shared. Today, much of what we know about the early history of Manistique and its people, we glean through the writings of its popular first newspaper editor, Wright E. Clarke—even though the man himself was an enigma.

There was nothing mysterious about the life of Captain Henry Bundy. Born into poverty in London, England in 1826, his parents indentured him at the tender age of ten to the captain of an ocean-going merchant vessel. After spending two decades sailing the world's oceans, Bundy was drawn to the American Great Lakes and the profits that could be made in the wheat trade. He settled in Chicago and while there he finally learned to read and write. There he also met and married a young Irish immigrant who became his devoted companion. Bundy lived the life of a sailor and was as rough and profane as any man on the sea, but after undergoing a conversion experience his life's course was altered completely. Giving up the merchant trade, Bundy dedicated himself to the selfless task of bringing the Gospel message to the isolated islands and villages along the shores of the Great Lakes. Bundy was a frequent summertime visitor to Manistique and other nearby ports during the 1880s and 90s, preaching from the deck of his Gospel ships and from the pulpit of local churches.

Another Great Lakes captain, Hermann Schuenemann, literally brought Christmas to thousands of children in Chicago each year in the form of Christmas trees from Thompson, Michigan. Both Hermann and his older brother, August, were drawn to Lake Michigan, and both lost their lives in November gales. Lake Michigan is often beautiful and enchanting, but it can also be treacherous and unforgiving. For the early pioneers the lake was their only link with the outside world, and the only means of obtaining supplies and selling their goods. Many of the stories in the *Hiawatha Anthology* demonstrate the central role the Great Lakes played in the lives of the early pioneers. The story of the Christmas tree ship brings home the dangers posed to those who sailed these waters, especially during the month of November.

The story of Maud Robbins in "The Lumberman's Daughter" spotlights the role of live theatre entertainment in the days before movies, radios or television. The early pioneers of central Upper Michigan patronized both home talent shows and traveling professional theatre troupes. Manistique was regularly visited by thespian groups such as the *James Browne Theatre Company* of Chicago, which toured small towns throughout the upper Midwest.

"The Lumberman's Daughter" also sheds light on the underside of domestic violence in the nineteenth century and one young woman's courageous struggle to escape its horrors. The abuser's mission to obtain power and control over his spouse was made much easier in the male dominated society of our ancestors. The theatre company paid the Robbins couple a joint salary which was totally controlled by Eugene Robbins. Maud was left destitute. If not for the assistance of her family, she might never have broken free from her tormentor. Many other women were not so fortunate.

The only person with few redeeming qualities profiled in *The Hiawatha Anthology* is that of Dan Heffron in "The Downfall of a Dive Keeper." For years, saloon and bawdy house owner, Dan Heffron, outsmarted the Chicago Lumbering Company bosses who were obsessed with keeping Manistique a dry community. The lumber company lost that battle, but when Dan continued to operate his bordello, even his brother the sheriff could not protect him. Once Michigan's Attorney General was sent to Manistique to take over the prosecution's case, Dan had no chance to prevail in court. Saloons, which also promoted gambling and prostitution, were common in lumbering boom towns of the nineteenth century and Manistique was no exception.

The timid fisherman, Augustus Pond, is featured in "Pond v. The People." The events which led up to the landmark Michigan Supreme Court ruling regarding self-defense, took place in June of 1859 on the rocky shore at Seul Choix Point in central Upper Michigan. The area attracted commercial fisherman from all over the eastern U.P. due to the great abundance of whitefish and lake trout in the waters off the point. The details of Pond's life before and after the shooting have been largely lost to history. Nevertheless, Pond's legacy continues on in the landmark case which bears his name.

"Utopia in the Northwoods" chronicles the life of Hiawatha farmer, Abe Byers. Byers was a deeply religious man who eagerly explored new horizons and new ways of looking at society. He was constantly agitating for change, often to the great annoyance of his neighbors. But, in 1893, when the country spiraled into a deep economic depression, Byers convinced an internationally known socialist activist and orator to come to Upper Michigan to help organize a cooperative community. Although doomed to failure, the short-lived social experiment offered an idealistic, albeit unattainable, solution to the severe economic hardships faced by farmers and laborers during the mid-1890s.

August Klagstad was only five years old when his family emigrated from Norway in May of 1871. A few months later, they settled in Manistique when the pioneer lumbering settlement was in its infancy. "Portrait of an Altar Artist" recounts the fascinating boyhood experiences of August Klagstad growing up in an isolated pioneer community. Klagstad's reminiscence provides a rare first-hand account of life in the remote 1870s community. When the Klagstad family first arrived, Manistique could not boast of a single school building or church. Consequently, Klagstad's mother provided her children with all their early religious and academic instruction, which took place in the Klagstad home and in their native Norwegian language. Klagstad's father spent 11 hours a day laboring in the mill earning just a dollar and a half per day. From these humble beginnings, August Klagstad would emerge as a prominent and prolific religious artist whose altar paintings adorned churches throughout the United States and around the world.

"The Pioneer Life of Elizabeth Allen" details the often unheralded role that women played in pioneer society. Allen was a young child when her parents moved to the remote wilderness of the Garden Peninsula in central Upper Michigan in the early 1860s. Being the oldest child, Elizabeth worked alongside her father in all phases of his commercial fishing enterprise. Later, when her father built a trading vessel for selling goods along the northern shore of Lake Michigan, Elizabeth went along. But perhaps her greatest adventure took place during the summer of 1868, when at age 15 she delivered the mail on horseback, through an uncharted primal forest.

"The Last Log Drive" highlights the event which marked the end of the white pine lumbering era. During the spring and early summer of 1929, the largest remaining stand of Michigan's virgin white pine floated down the Manistique River. The careers of pioneer woodsmen Frank Cookson and his nephew Harvey Saunders are featured in this saga about big pine lumbering during the latter half of the nineteenth century.

"Jamestown" relates the story of Ebenezer James, a lumberman with Quaker roots, who arrived in Monistique in the mid-1870s from Oshkosh, Wisconsin. The Jamestown settlement quickly sprang to life on the banks of the Monistique River and for a brief time eclipsed its sister city of Manistique. But poor geography and stiff competition doomed the enterprise and by 1885 the settlement was a ghost town. Jamestown epitomizes the boom and bust nature of the white pine lumbering era. No trace of its existence can be seen today.

The French explorer, Robert Cavalier de LaSalle, arrived at Michilimackinac on present day Mackinac Island during August of 1679. He came on the brig Griffin—the first sailing vessel to ever traverse the Great Lakes. The Griffin's sailing career was brief, lasting less than a year before disappearing in September of 1679. "The Voyage of the Griffin" chronicles the life of the ship and the search for clues regarding its final resting place, which continues to this day.

Other pioneers highlighted in this anthology include a cobbler; a Methodist circuit rider; a lighthouse keeper; an ice cream store owner; a family of lawmen; and finally, a merchant whose greatest legacy is the conservation of a natural wonder.

It is my hope that these stories will provide the reader with a glimpse into a not so distant past before technology, when life was simpler but also more perilous and uncertain. Modern medical advances were decades away and life expectancy was short. Though the times were different, the people themselves were very much like us. They were just as alive as we are today—with the same emotions and the same enduring hopes and aspirations for themselves and their children. Their struggles and that of thousands of others like them, laid the foundation for the lives we have today.

Chapter One:
A Strange Tale of Two Editors

The burgeoning lumber town of Manistique on the northern shore of Lake Michigan was the scene in the 1880s of a spirited newspaper rivalry unlike any other. The opposing newspaper editors were well liked and respected figures in the community. They also shared a scandalous secret that would not be made public until after their deaths.

Civil War veteran, Major Wright E. Clarke, came to Upper Michigan in 1877 from LaGrange, Ohio. Clarke settled first in Escanaba before arriving in Manistique with his wife Alice and their five-year-old daughter Mattie in April 1880.

During his early years in Schoolcraft County, the major was elected to several positions of public trust, including the Office of Probate Judge and Commissioner of the Circuit Court. Clarke also began the publication of a weekly newspaper, the *Schoolcraft County Pioneer*. The first edition of the *Pioneer* was published on April 29, 1880.[1] Clarke owned and edited the paper from its founding until his death in 1896. He advocated for civic improvements in the fast-growing town, such as the organization of a fire department, better streets and sidewalks, and a new jail to deter the lawless element. Clarke spoke out against the drunkenness, vice and corruption which prevailed in the booming lumber region of that era. During the spring of 1883 Clarke took a stand against a local "bawdy house" and the illegal sale of strong liquor. As a result, he narrowly escaped assassination. On May 7, 1883 he was shot at through an open window in his office while he wrote at his desk. The bullet grazed the fingers of his left hand. Later that year, the newspaper building was destroyed by arson.[2]

---

1   "Our Fiftieth Anniversary," *Manistique Pioneer Tribune,* May 8, 1930, p.1. See also "Alice W. Clark Dies Yesterday" *Escanaba Daily Press,* May 11, 1934, p.13. See also August Klagstad *Klagstad-Halvorsen Family History* (Minneapolis, Minnesota, January 1946) p. 37.
2   "A Strange Life Ended," *Kokomo Dispatch,* May 27, 1896, p.4, c.1. See also "Our Fiftieth Anniversary," *Manistique Pioneer-Tribune,* May 8, 1930 p.1.

Clarke had a charismatic personality. His friends recalled that he was almost always pleasant and cheerful. He befriended those who were down on their luck and tried to assist them in making a fresh start. His humor and wit were two of his most endearing qualities. Clarke used those traits to comment about rumors that the railroad would soon be coming to Manistique:

"Everything grows in this climate that is planted. Just plant a very small grain of railroad news and in two days it will increase in size until a stranger would at once begin to inquire the way to the depot."[3]

Major Clarke actively participated in civic groups. He was a member of the Grand Army of the Republic post and served in various capacities including Chaplin and Post Commander.[4] He publicized the post's meetings and campfires in the *Pioneer*. When the "Sons of Veterans" Camp in Manistique was organized in February 1890, it was named W.E. Clarke Camp 202 in his honor. Clarke was also a leader in the local Good Templars society that promoted the Temperance cause.

In the early 1880s a young newspaperman from Indiana arrived in Manistique while traveling with a theatre troupe. His name was William (Will) Montgomery. During a walk around town, he spied a familiar figure on the streets of Manistique. A few days later Will Montgomery went to the *Pioneer* office where he introduced himself to his runaway father, Wright Clarke. The son had discovered his father years earlier when the major was living in LaGrange, Ohio but maintained his silence then to spare his family additional heartache. Now he stumbled upon his father again, this time living in Manistique. Major Clarke was courteous and acknowledged privately that Will Montgomery was his son. Clarke refused to talk about his former life in Indiana and gave no explanation for his desertion of his family. Little else is known of the conversation between father and son but they agreed to keep Clarke's true identity a secret.[5] In addition, Will Montgomery was hired to join the *Pioneer* workforce.

Clarke's real name was Seymour T. Montgomery. He was born in France in July 1820 and immigrated to New York with his parents as a small

---

3   *Semi-Weekly Pioneer,* March 9, 1886 p.1
4   Records of the George F. Fuller Post, Grand Army of the Republic, Library of Michigan, Lansing, MI.
5   "Odd Story of an Editor" *Omaha World Herald,* April 6, 1901, p.9

child.[6] He later relocated to Indiana where in 1856 he married Elizabeth Sipe. The couple had four children.[7] Seymour Montgomery fought in both the Mexican and Civil Wars. In 1861 he enlisted in the Twentieth Indiana Infantry, serving as a private and sergeant in Company I, before being promoted to hospital steward for the entire regiment (though never a major as he claimed).[8] His regiment served with distinction, suffering severe losses at Gettysburg in 1863. While in the army, the loquacious soldier wrote a series of letters which were printed in Kokomo's newspaper, *The Howard Tribune*. He was honorably discharged in October 1864. Following the war Montgomery returned to Kokomo, Indiana where he rejoined his family and entered the newspaper business, partnering with T. C. Phillips as editor of the *Kokomo Tribune*. The popular new publisher was elected to the state legislature and was also a prominent leader in the temperance movement. He was selected as "Grand Worthy Chief Templar" representing all the Good Templar lodges in the State of Indiana.

**William F. Montgomery,
courtesy Susan Cucchiarella**

In 1870 he and his family moved to Mishawaka, Indiana where he became editor of the *Mishawaka Enterprise*. The former editor of the paper, Norman Brower, had opposed a tax levy designed to entice an additional east-west running railroad to come through Mishawaka to compete with the existing *Lake Shore Road* railway. Seymour T. Montgomery's uncle, Robert Montgomery, who owned a wagon manufacturing company, was a proponent of the tax levy. So when the vote went against the railroad, the uncle blamed the newspaper and started a campaign to drive its editor out of town. Once Robert Montgomery wrestled

---

6   Sipe Family Bible, Kokomo Indiana Public Library, Kokomo, Indiana. See also 1870 United States Census, City of Kokomo, Howard County Indiana, Household
7   Schoolcraft County Probate Court Archives, Estate of Wright E. Clarke (Marriage License dated July 18, 1856). See also Sipe Family Bible, Kokomo Public Library, Kokomo, Indiana
8   National Archives, Seymour T. Montgomery Civil War Pension Index, Application number 643764

control of the paper from Brower, he summoned his nephew to become its new editor.[9]

> **An Editor Missing.**
>
> S. T. Montgomery, editor of the Mishawaka *Enterprise*, is missing and we learn that no paper will be issued from that office this week. The last seen of Mr. Montgomery was at the fire here on Monday evening. His friends are greatly alarmed concerning his fate. We hope he may yet turn up safe and sound.—*South Bend Tribune* June 22nd.
>
> We have learned since, that serious complications and financial difficulties, were the main incentives to the taking off so suddenly the head of the concern at Mishawaka. A relative, who as we are told, was the sole proprietor of the office of the *Enterprise*, found it was running into the ground, under the administration of S. T., and so concluded to shut down and stop until it could be conducted with a little more economy.
>
> *Democratic Union* newspaper, Elkhart, Indiana, June 28, 1872, p.2, c.5.

The *Enterprise* gave every appearance of thriving under the leadership of its handsome and popular new editor, Seymour T. Montgomery. Increases in the newspaper's circulation and job printing contracts necessitated a move to a larger office and an increase in the size of the paper.[10] To attract even more readers, he lowered the subscription cost to $1.50 per year.[11] Always a hard worker, the energetic Montgomery still found time to travel throughout Indiana lecturing on behalf of the Temperance cause. On June 17, 1872, the editor was seen at the terrible fire that engulfed the Studebaker Wagon Factory in nearby South Bend, Indiana. In the confusion he inexplicably vanished from the scene.[12] Initial reports stated that Montgomery had perished in the flames, but when the debris was cleared away no trace of his remains was found. Montgomery's friends feared that he had "fallen into the hands of thieves and murderers."[13] But as the true state of the economic affairs of the *Mishawaka Enterprise* was uncovered, nearly everyone concluded that the editor had fled to avoid financial ruin.

Montgomery's sister-in-law, Mrs. John Sipe, testified that Montgomery was always pleasant and kind to his family. On the morning of his disappearance, he kissed his wife and three children good bye, saying he was going to South Bend for a couple of days to "raise some money."

9   "The Remarkable Careers of Two Indiana Newspaper Men" *The Goshen Democrat,* December 30, 1891
10   *The Goshen Democrat,* March 15, 1871, p3,c2.
11   *Democratic Union,* Elkhart, Indiana, July 12, 1872, p2c5.
12   "S.T. Montgomery Discovered After Five Years" *The Kokomo Saturday Tribune,* May 26, 1877
13   *The Cambridge City Tribune,* Cambridge City, Indiana, July 18, 1872

His wife would never see him again.[14] At the time of his disappearance Montgomery left his wife Elizabeth and three minor children; two-year-old Robert; Truman, age five and William, age 14 without any means of support. The couple's only daughter, May Montgomery, died in infancy in 1861 while her father was serving in the army. The editor's wife Elizabeth returned with her family to the couple's former home in Kokomo, Indiana, unsure what to believe about her husband's fate. Friends and relatives claimed that she never gave up hope that he would return. She kept a candle burning every night in her front window to lead him home. Broken-hearted, Elizabeth died on January 28, 1876, still grieving for her absent husband.

After the Montgomery family returned to Kokomo in 1872, T.C. Phillips, editor of the *Kokomo Tribune,* hired 14-year-old Will Montgomery as a typesetter. The boy was so small that he had to stand on a high box to reach the upper rack, but the money he earned helped support his family.[15]

Five years later, word reached Will Montgomery that someone recognized his father living in LaGrange, Lorain County, Ohio. He left immediately for LaGrange to determine for himself if his father was alive. The young Montgomery found his father living in the town under the assumed name of Edwin W. Clark. Clark's charismatic personality had so inspired the trust of his fellow townspeople that they elected him mayor. He also was local editor of the *LaGrange Journal* and served as a correspondent for the *Elyria Republican.* Clark married for the second time on August 13, 1873 to Alice Wood of LaGrange, while still legally married to his first wife, Elizabeth.[16] This new union produced one child. Clark told his second bride that he was previously married but claimed that his first wife and their three children had all died in a scarlet fever epidemic.[17] In May of 1877 the editor of the *Kokomo Tribune* wrote that the elder "Montgomery could deceive angels and make them believe him more holy than they."[18]

---

14 National Archives, Civil War Pension File of Seymour T. Montgomery A.K.A. Wright E. Clarke, Deposition of Mrs. John (Elizabeth) Sipe, January 17, 1903.
15 "The Remarkable Careers of Two Indiana Newspaper Men" *The Goshen Democrat,* December 30, 1891
16 Schoolcraft County Probate Court Archives, Estate of Wright E. Clarke (Marriage Certificate dated Aug 13, 1873)
17 United States Congressional Serial Set, 58th Congress, 2nd Session, pp. 816-818, Alice W. Clarke.
18 "S.T. Montgomery Discovered After Five Years" *The Kokomo Saturday Tribune,* May 26, 1877

After meeting with his father in LaGrange, Will Montgomery returned to Kokomo. He denied that his father was living in the Ohio town. The young newspaper man may have kept his father's secret to spare his orphan brothers additional anguish. The family had been split apart after their mother's death in 1876. Robbie was sent to live with a relative in Illinois while Truman moved to an aunt's home in Michigan. Will Montgomery remained in Kokomo, living with his uncle, John Sipe.

Alice Wood Clarke with daughter Mattie, circa 1877. Schoolcraft County Historical Society photo, MacLeod Family Collection

Clark was eventually exposed in LaGrange when someone sent a letter to the newspaper with photos of the elder Montgomery enclosed. After the letter was published in the *Elyria Constitution* on May 22, 1877, Clark skipped town. The son did not see his father again until their meeting in Manistique.

Will Montgomery lived in Manistique for almost nine years. In July of 1883, he was made foreman of the "mechanical department" of the *Pioneer* and also was given responsibility for covering some of the local items of the day. In making the announcement, Clarke described his new employee as a "master workman" and a "good writer with enough energy to move things forward."[19]

The new foreman was soon called upon to assume even more responsibility for the daily operation and editorial voice of the *Pioneer*. In the months following the destruction of the *Pioneer* office by arson in late December of 1883, Major Clarke was diagnosed as suffering from lead poisoning. His symptoms included severe muscle weakness in his arms and hands. Hospitalized in Cleveland, his doctors prescribed complete rest to effect a cure. Thus incapacitated, the management of the

19 *Schoolcraft County Pioneer,* June 28, 1883, p.3.

Pioneer fell to Clarke's foreman, Will Montgomery and Clarke's wife, Alice.[20] Montgomery immediately took up his father's torch opposing vice and intemperance. In the Major's absence, the *Pioneer's* editorial denunciation of the county's lawbreakers became even more spirited and confrontational. The *Pioneer* would take no backward steps while its founder was away. Once his condition improved, Clarke was able to resume his editorial duties.

In October of 1885, Will Montgomery left the *Pioneer* and established The *Sunday Sun,* which he ran in opposition to his father's paper. The *Sun's* inspiring motto proclaimed "It shines for all." The advent of a rival newspaper in Manistique was reported on the front page of the *Pioneer.*

"The first number of Mr. Montgomery's new newspaper appeared last Sunday and was distributed freely about town in time to be read at the early breakfast table. It is the same size as THE PIONEER, printed on new type, well filled with reading material and edited with ability. It is mechanically neat, and gives the telegraphic news up to a late hour Saturday night. It is just such a paper as we knew "Mont." would print; and we hope his most sanguine financial anticipations may be realized. If we must have a competitor, we want a *live* one; just what THE SUN undoubted will be."[21]

Elyria Ohio *Constitution* article dated May 22, 1877

The rival editors attended public meetings and were active in the social events of the town. They joined fraternal organizations including the Good Templars and the Knights of Pythias. During these gatherings they always treated each other with politeness and respect. No one suspected they were

---

20 "Special Notice" *Schoolcraft County Pioneer,* March 8, 1884, p.2.
21 "The Sun" *Semi-Weekly Pioneer,* October 6, 1885, p.1

father and son. The editors confined their competition to the columns of their papers. The *Pioneer* was an ardently Republican newspaper while the *Sunday Sun* was registered as an Independent weekly. The editors vigorously attacked the political policies advocated by the other but avoided personal assaults on the other's honor or integrity.

Mary McCanna Montgomery, courtesy Susan Cucchiarella Collection

The rival editors carried on an unusual business relationship. Major Clarke quietly assisted his son in his newspaper enterprise. The *Sun* was located for a time in the same building as the *Pioneer* but with a separate entrance from the street. A door in the center of the building marked "employees only" separated the two offices.[22] When emergencies required it, the *Sun* was published using the *Pioneer* presses.[23] The father also discreetly arranged for a portion of the county's printing contracts to be given to the *Sun*.[24]

While he resided in Manistique, Will Montgomery married and started a family. He wed Mary McCanna, younger sister of the county sheriff, John McCanna, at a ceremony in Manistique on July 2, 1882. Their first child, Theo, was born on December 5, 1887. Will Montgomery, who had inherited his father's humor and wit, was well-liked in the community. He was described by one contemporary as being "very picturesque." He always carried two pistols and fittingly served several terms as "Master of Arms" of the Knights of Pythias lodge.[25] The civic minded young editor also volunteered as a fireman on the city's horse drawn "hook and ladder" truck.[26] The hook and ladder truck is on display

22 *Semi-Weekly Pioneer,* November 3, 1885, p.1
23 *Semi-Weekly Pioneer,* March 9, 1886, p.1
24 "Odd Story of an Editor" *Omaha World Herald,* April 6, 1901, p.9
25 "Carl Thorborg Honored by Knights of Pythias on 50th Anniversary" *Escanaba Daily Press,* March 6, 1938, p.13
26 "Wedding Bells" *The Sunday Sun,* July 4, 1886, p.1

at Pioneer Park in Manistique.

Will Montgomery remained in Manistique until 1890 when circumstances forced him to give up the unequal competition with the popular Clarke and the *Pioneer*. The deck had always been stacked against him. The *Pioneer* was supported by loyal readers and advertisers, making it difficult for the *Sun* to carve out a solid base of subscribers and businessmen willing to purchase commercial space in its pages. By late 1889 the *Sun's* readership and advertisers had dwindled to the point that Montgomery was left with little choice but to shut the paper down. No longer able to pay the mortgage on the printing office or the salaries of his employees, he teetered on the edge of bankruptcy.

Image courtesy the Schoolcraft Co. Probate Court archives

The stress related to the failure of his newspaper and his inability to support his family triggered an onset of mental illness. Suffering a psychotic break, Montgomery experienced terrifying visual hallucinations and delusions. At times he imagined that he was horribly maimed with his hands and feet cut off. At other times he believed that his son Theo was dead or that his house was on fire. His most prominent delusion was that he was still running a newspaper, sending and receiving telegrams and telephone messages. He exhibited episodes of violence and had to be physically restrained.[27] Clarke provided updates in the *Pioneer* on the condition "of the editor of the *Sun.*" Recalling Montgomery's days at the *Pioneer,* Clarke praised his son "as one of the best newspaper men we

---

27 Schoolcraft County Probate Court Archives, In The Matter of Will F. Montgomery, Affidavit of Mary M. Montgomery, November 24, 1889

ever had in our employ."[28] Clarke believed his son's illness was caused by physical and mental exhaustion related to running his newspaper.

> "He had to work night and day, exposed himself in visiting [lumber] camps, etc., and the result is, while still a young man, a broken-down constitution and a mind badly wrecked, if not wholly ruined. Rumor has many other excuses for this condition of affairs, some plausible, others silly. We have no desperation to print any of them and certainly not since he was our competitor in business. We earnestly hope for his speedy recovery from this terrible and heart-rending sickness."[29]

On November 29, 1889, Will Montgomery was committed to the Northern Michigan Asylum in Traverse City, Michigan. He remained institutionalized for eight weeks before finally regaining his hold on reality. When he returned to Manistique he found his printing office sold to cover his many debts.

In 1890, Will Montgomery and his family moved to the Upper Peninsula mining town of Republic, Michigan. There he started another paper, the *Republic Sun*. In this new venture, he was associated with Will Hubbard Kernan, former editor of a Mississippi newspaper known for its "intensely erratic and fire-eating" editorials.[30] Montgomery immediately distinguished his newspaper through his advocacy for separate statehood for the Upper Peninsula.[31] He also bitterly opposed the saloons and bordellos which flourished in the pioneer mining town. The *Sun's* editorials were so strident and unflagging that it was feared that the proprietors of these "dens of iniquity" would seek retribution.

Tragedy struck in September of 1891. The editor and his family, including a new baby boy, lived on the upper floor of the newspaper building. A fire, believed caused by the explosion of a lamp in the printing office, quickly spread to the living quarters. Montgomery was critically injured while rescuing his infant son from the flames. He died a few days later but his wife and children survived unharmed.

A short time before his death, Will Montgomery wrote a letter to a

28 "Sad" *Tri-Weekly Pioneer*, November 30, 1889 p.1
29 Ibid.
30 "The Remarkable Careers of Two Indiana Newspaper Men" *The Goshen Democrat*, December 30, 1891
31 *Superior, A State For The North Country*, James L. Carter, The Pilot Press, Marquette, MI. 1980; See also, *Sault Ste. Marie News*, August 12, 1892, p.2

friend in Kokomo, Indiana detailing his father's double life and his own relationship with his father as a rival newspaper editor in Manistique. In the letter he explained why he had kept his father's true identity a secret.

> "Nor would it have been any satisfaction to me to expose him at Manistique when I found him there as editor of the *Pioneer*, for the wrong that he had done could not then be righted, and I would only have called attention to conditions that no mortal could remedy, and probably invoked defense on his part that I could not successfully deny though I might believe it untrue. For this reason I held my peace and expect to do so to the end."[32]

He left instructions that the secret of Clarke's true identity be made known only after his father's death.

The news of the fire at the *Republic Sun* newspaper office made front page headlines in the *Pioneer*. Initial reports indicated that Montgomery's injuries were not severe. Major Clarke was openly supportive.

> "The news "finds many sympathizers here and none more so than the *Pioneer* force with whom Mr. M. was associated several years ago. He has worked hard to build up a paper and a home, but now it is in ashes. It is hard to see the accumulations of years thus swept away. We hope the people of Republic will at once rally to the rescue of Mr. M. and see that he is at once put in possession of a new office. He has done much for the benefit of that town, and now that he is crippled he should receive backing to start in business again at once. The family will please accept the writer's sympathy for the loss that has befallen them."[33]

The true magnitude of the tragedy reached the *Pioneer* office by telegram five days later. The brief dispatch read as follows; "Will is dead! Died this morning from injuries received at the fire. Mrs. W. F. Montgomery."[34]

Even in death, Clarke could not bring himself to publicly acknowledge the true relationship between himself and Will Montgomery. Nonetheless, Clarke did extol his former rival's virtues in the pages of the *Pioneer*.

---

32 "Odd Story of an Editor" *Omaha World Herald,* April 6, 1901 p.9
33 "A Disastrous Scorching! 'Republic Sun' Office Burned" *Tri-Weekly Pioneer,* September 24, 1891 p.1
34 "W. F. Montgomery Dead" *Tri-Weekly Pioneer,* September 29, 1891 p.1

The only known image of Wright Clarke is a group photo of Civil War veterans during the 1880s. Clarke is the fifth from the right, with his head down buttoning his coat. Photo courtesy the Schoolcraft County Historical Society.

> "He was a man of many noble traits, as an editor he was fearless in his attacks, but had many friends. He made some mistakes in life, but his heroic death should wipe out the memory of all errors, and now that he is gone, let us only remember his openheartedness, his devotion to family and friends." [35]

During the fall of 1893 Clarke met his youngest son, Robert M. Montgomery, in Manistique. Robert stayed in a hotel in Manistique for over a month and did some work around the *Pioneer* office. He also demanded financial assistance in exchange for his silence concerning their true relationship. During this time, he had several conversations with his father and he asked Clarke why he had abandoned his family.

> "I asked him the reason he left us in the way he did, and he said he did not feel that he had done anything wrong; he

[35] *Tri-Weekly Pioneer,* October 3, 1891 p.1

always declined to give the reason. At another time telling of his past life, he came to the point of telling me the reason, but changed off into something else. I brought him back to that subject and asked him a direct question, what was the reason he left us in the condition he did, and he said if he would tell me that it would make my bones ache. I told him they could not ache any worse than they had over it, but he changed the subject again and would not talk about it."[36]

Clarke also had a meeting with his other son, Truman Montgomery, in Cheboygan, Michigan. Clarke readily agreed to assist both sons financially including paying for all of Robert's tuition and board at Otterbein School of Theology, but the sons' timing could not have been worse. The financial "Panic of 1893" had brought hard times to Manistique and money was tight. But the demands for more cash and threats to "clear up dark mysteries for the people of Manistique" continued from both sons up until the time of Clarke's death.[37]

Clarke suffered "an attack of paralysis" in 1894, but recovered sufficiently to perform some of his editorial duties. He was no longer able to set type and was forced to write with his right hand. He was unable to work much of the time. Near the end of his life Clarke finally told his wife Alice the truth about his identity and his previous marriage.

Wright Clarke died on May 22, 1896 at age 75. Within a week of his death, newspapers in Indiana and across the country carried the story revealed in Will Montgomery's letter to his friend in Kokomo. Clarke's last will and testament was filed in the Schoolcraft County Probate Court on September 6, 1896. His wife, Alice Clarke, was named the beneficiary. The surviving children of Major Clarke's first marriage unsuccessfully contested the will. Meanwhile, the citizens of Manistique reassessed the life of the man they thought they knew and had so admired. A memorial to Major Clarke written a year after his death by J. H. MacNaughton, editor of *The Manistique Courier* observed:

> ... "[Clarke] lived a moral, charitable and upright life in this community during the many years he spent working for

---

36 Schoolcraft County Probate Court Archives, The Estate of Wright E. Clarke, Deposition of Robert M. Montgomery, September 22, 1896

37 Schoolcraft County Probate Court Archives, The Estate of Wright E. Clarke, Letter from Virgil Hixson, Attorney, to Truman Montgomery dated May 18, 1896 and Letter from Virgil Hixson, Attorney, to Robert Montgomery dated May 28, 1896.

its welfare and whatever clouds may have shadowed his path under other skies, and in other times and places, his life here was beyond reproach and an example worthy of all emulation, no one ever doubted his sincerity and no one ever questioned his earnestness of purpose or his desire to help, aid and assist his fellow creatures. ... 'After I am dead, think of me not as I was, but as you know I wished to be,' was a request made by him to this writer shortly before his death."[38]

Will Montgomery's widow moved back to Manistique with her two sons, Theo and William. She married George Moody on December 18, 1900.

In November of 1896, Alice Clarke applied for a widow's pension based on her husband's Civil War service. Her application was initially denied on the grounds that a valid marriage with Wright Clarke did not exist. The decision was ultimately reversed by a special act of Congress based on the testimony of Alice Clarke. She stated that at the time of her marriage in 1873, she was unaware that her husband was legally married to someone else. Still believing that Clarke's first family had perished in a scarlet fever epidemic, she claimed that she did not learn of his bigamy until a year before his death.

The lives of Will Montgomery and his father Wright Clarke were notable both for their similarities and their contrasts. Although only one issue of the *Sunday Sun* has survived, both men were obviously talented newspaper editors. Montgomery's short-lived *Republic Sun* won much acclaim from his fellow Upper Peninsula editors. Father and son were both civic minded and advocated for improvements in the communities where they lived.

The starkest contrast between the two men was in their personal lives. Clarke took advantage of the opportunity presented by a terrible fire to desert his family and start a second life. On the other hand, Will Montgomery sacrificed his own life to rescue his family from a fire that destroyed both his newspaper office and his home.

Clarke never revealed the reason he deserted his family in Indiana. The act was completely out of character for him. Perhaps he was compelled to

---

38 "In Memoriam" *The Manistique Courier,* May 7, 1897

leave the scene by enemies made through his newspaper editorials, or by an episode of mental illness which later afflicted his son. Rumors alleged illicit affairs and financial mismanagement, but neither explanation is very convincing. As for Clarke, he took any explanations with him to his grave.

Chapter Two:
Captain Bundy and his Gospel Ships

Foul and irreverent, Henry Bundy embodied the popular image of the nineteenth century sailor. His career as a mariner, begun at age 10, carried him to the world's exotic ports. After 30 years in the merchant trade, his life took an astonishing turn. Converted to Christianity, he gained enduring fame as the sailor missionary of the upper Great Lakes.

Captain Henry Bundy, Sue Baar Collection

Henry Bundy was born in England in 1826 to impoverished parents. He spent his early childhood roaming the streets of London, never attending school. When Henry was 10 years old his father imposed a harsh discipline. He bound his rebellious son for seven years as an apprentice to the captain of the *Abel Gower,* a three-masted, 313 ton merchant ship.[1]

Henry's first sea voyage took him from London, around the tip of Africa, to the port of Bombay, India. The passage was grueling. The crew ran short of drinking water and the ships remaining supply was strictly rationed. When Henry was caught by his shipmates stealing water, his seaman's education was begun. Though merely a boy, he was tied to the mast and lashed with a whip.[2] The *Abel Gower's* round trip voyage to Bombay took 14 months. His next journey was to Quebec, Canada. During

---

1 *Beeson's Marine Directory of the Northwestern Lakes*, Harvey Child Beeson, Eleventh Edition, Chicago, Ill., 1898, Page 194 ; See also, *Lloyd's Register of Shipping 1831,* London, England, 1831, Page 6

2 *"Capt. Bundy Makes His Last Port" Duluth News Tribune,* Duluth, Minnesota, September 24, 1906, Pg. 7

his sailing career he visited six continents including Australia. Bundy even served a two-year hitch in the British Navy.[3]

Bundy spent over two decades sailing the world's oceans, but he could not resist the lure of the American Great Lakes and the profits to be made in the wheat trade. In 1858 Bundy sailed to Chicago, Illinois and made that city his home. Bundy was an expert seaman, but had no formal education. During the winter months, he attended night classes and learned to read and write. In 1863 he married Margaret McCredie, an immigrant from Ireland, who became his devoted companion. Their union produced three children, Henry, Agnes and Maggie.

Margaret Bundy,
Sue Baar Collection

During the 1860s Bundy sailed on a number of merchant vessels based in Great Lakes ports including the schooner *George Foot* of Detroit. He became part owner of the schooner *Henry Hager* before finally being able to purchase his own ship, the bark *Potomac* which he sailed as captain.[4]

Bundy lived the life of a sailor and was as rough and profane as any man on the seas. He was powerfully built and never backed down from a fight. In 1869 he underwent a transformation that left his friends amazed. While the *Potomac* was tied up to the dock at Halsted Street in Chicago, some women from the nearby Free Methodist Church asked permission to come aboard and hold religious services in the captain's cabin. Bundy reluctantly agreed. He loved music and the Methodist hymns delighted him so much that he asked the women to return. Within a short time, the captain became a believer.[5]

Bundy felt obligated to spread the Gospel and he began with the crew of the *Potomac,* all nine of whom were converted to Christianity. Bundy quit the merchant trade and dedicated his life to preaching the Word to Great Lakes sailors, fishermen and lumbermen. The *Potomac* became a missionary vessel and flew the Bethel flag which identified her as a floating chapel. But the ship was ill suited for this purpose.

Bundy gave up the seafaring life for a time in the early 1870s. He

3   *Duluth News Tribune,* September 24, 1906, Page 7
4   *Beeson's Marine Directory of the Northwestern Lakes,* Harvey Child Beeson, Page 194
5   *Duluth News Tribune,* September 24, 1906, Page 7

preached in Chicago at the Mariner's Hospital and among the sailors on the docks. He also had a wagon stand which he used to preach on the street corners. Often Bundy would be greeted with missiles of rotten eggs, spoiled potatoes and over-ripe fruit. But eventually the abuse ceased-- "The people come to know me and didn't fire nothing at me" Bundy explained.[6]

In 1876 Captain Bundy received $500 and the endorsement of the Western Seaman's Friends Society to outfit a vessel to conduct religious services in the isolated settlements and islands along the northern shores of Lake Michigan.[7] Bundy purchased an old life boat which he had outfitted into a Bethel ship. He named her the *Glad Tidings*.

The hull of the 23 foot, 5 ton *Glad Tidings* was painted black with the image of an open Bible across her stern.[8] A six foot tall cabin adorned her deck. Bundy had personally supervised the construction and used the design of English life boats as a model. She was launched in June, 1876, on a Friday, which was considered a bad omen among sailors. The tradition of breaking a bottle of wine at her christening was also ignored.[9] After taking on a cargo of Bibles and religious pamphlets, Bundy set out from Chicago on July 17, 1876. A reporter covering the event did not think the little craft was seaworthy: "The boat is a schooner, with her mainmast situated most too far aft for any good in a heavy sea. Her foremast is too short for bad weather, and taken in all, the boat is the worst that possibly could be built for the shifting winds of the lake."[10]

Bundy's excursion in the summer of 1876 took him to several remote villages where he established Sunday schools and gave out Bibles. He traveled as far as Menominee, stopping along the way at Green Bay, Port Washington and Washington Island. He returned safe and sound to Chicago on October 21, 1876.[11]

Bundy had a new ship built for his 1877 missionary cruise and she was also christened the *Glad Tidings*. The second *Glad Tidings* was built at Chicago at a cost of $1,700 from funds received from Christian benefactors.[12] The new ship was a two-masted, 40-foot, 33-ton sloop.

6 " A Salvation Sailor," *Buffalo Courier,* Buffalo, New York, April 27, 1886
7 "A Missionary Vessel," *The Daily Inter-Ocean,* Chicago, Illinois, April 26, 1876, Page 7
8 *The Chicago Tribune,* Chicago, Illinois, June 12, 1876, Page 6
9 "The Gospel Ship. Launch of the Glad Tidings" *The Chicago Tribune,* June 24, 1876, Page 8
10 "The 'Good Tidings,' Bidding Her Farwell" *The Chicago Tribune,* July 18, 1876, Page 7
11 *The Chicago Tribune,* October 21, 1876, Page 8
12 "The Two Glad Tidings" *The Chicago Tribune,* June 9, 1877, Page 7

The cabin was large enough to accommodate Bundy's family along with an altar and melodeon. Bundy's wife Margaret played hymns on the melodeon while his children cheerfully passed the hat for collection. A tent was stored for use during onshore services.

The Glad Tidings in Sault Ste. Marie, Chippewa County Historical Society, Bayliss Public Library

Bundy preached in the "hellfire and brimstone" style of that era. He warned his alarmed listeners about the consequences of sin and showed them the way to salvation. Bundy's sermons were non-denominational. "We never say anything about any church," he once said, "but keep preaching the love of Christ."[13] His missionary voyage of 1877 took him as far as Beaver Island. Bundy's endeavors were most successful in the South Manitou island group and on St. Martin's Island where he had many converts. The *Glad Tidings* returned to Chicago on November 1, 1877.[14]

Captain Bundy's missionary efforts did not go unacknowledged. He was ordained an evangelist in June of 1878 at a ceremony in Chicago by the Western Seaman's Friend Society.[15]

The *Glad Tidings* had spent the winter of 1879 in Buffalo, New York. She embarked on her annual missionary cruise on June 14 and arrived at the Straits of Mackinac on July 3. From Mackinac, Bundy headed to Sault Ste. Marie and preached for three consecutive evenings to large crowds in

13 "The Sailor Preacher" *The Sentinel,* Milwaukee, Wisconsin, March 23, 1891, Page 3
14 "Captain Bundy's Cruise" *The Daily Inter-Ocean,* November 30, 1877, Page 8
15 *The Chicago Tribune,* June 6, 1878, Page 9

outdoor services. He carried a cargo of Bibles in five different languages: French, Danish, Norwegian, German and English.[16] When a family was too poor to purchase a Bible, Bundy gave them one as a gift. From Sault Ste. Marie the little vessel headed out on Lake Superior, stopping for a week at Marquette before sailing on to Hancock and the Apostle Islands. Bundy traveled as far west as Superior, Wisconsin and Duluth, Minnesota. On the return voyage the *Glad Tidings* stopped at communities all along the southern Lake Superior shore, before finally going into winter quarters at Cheboygan on Lake Huron.[17] The captain preached sermons, gave out materials to establish Sunday schools, performed baptisms, and officiated at marriage ceremonies.

No port was too big or too small to escape Bundy's attention. He stopped at them all. One of his frequent visiting places was the thriving inlet at Sac Bay on the western shore of the Garden Peninsula. Services at Sac Bay were held in the local one-room school house—men and boys seated on the left and women and girls on the right. Bundy's enthusiastic singing left a lasting impression on those attending the worship. During a visit in October, 1891, a young girl had died of consumption (tuberculosis) and there was no minister to preach the funeral service. Bundy immediately volunteered and traveled the five miles to the girl's home to conduct the burial.[18]

Bundy believed the hand of Providence guided his ship. When the *Glad Tidings* ran aground in shallow water off Les Cheneaux Island in northern Lake Huron, Bundy refused assistance from local sailors to free his ship. The captain told them: "God put me here, and when He wants me to leave He will float my ship for me." Bundy conducted services for several days at the mainland village of Cedarville until a storm "floated" his ship and he was able to sail away.[19]

The local press was not always sympathetic to the captain. In September of 1879 the *Glad Tidings* came to Ontonagon where the captain held Sunday services in the Presbyterian Church. A reporter for the *Ontonagon Miner* observed that when Captain Bundy took up a collection to replenish his flour barrel which was running low, "many of his listeners could have

---

16 *The Sentinel*, March 23, 1891, Page 3

17 "The Gospel Ship. Her Cruise This Past Season" *The Daily Inter-Ocean,* December 19, 1879, Page 7

18 "Capt. Bundy Never Associated With Any Religious Denomination" *The Evening News,* Sault Ste. Marie, Michigan, September 4, 1952, Page 8

19 *The Evening News,* September 4, 1952, Page 8

told the same story."[20]

During the off season the captain was not idle. He spent his days at the Chicago docks, holding outdoor services for the unconverted sailors and longshoremen. The captain's exhortations were often met with jeers and ridicule but he carried on unperturbed.

Captain Bundy's missionary zeal sometimes ran afoul of the civil authorities. During the spring of 1887 Bundy stopped at the town of Kenosha, Wisconsin, on his way to the upper lakes. He set up at the corner of Main & Market Streets and began singing "in a good strong voice." This attracted a crowd and also the police. The officers objected to the congregation of people on the sidewalk. They were unfamiliar with the evangelist and mistook him for a crackpot. Bundy's explanations did not clarify the situation, but instead resulted in his arrest. Fortunately, his friends intervened and secured the captain's release.[21]

On June 10, 1883 the third *Glad Tidings* was launched from the ship yard at Manitowoc, Wisconsin.[22] She was a 50 ton, 113 foot schooner and was purchased through donations at a cost of $6000. Captain Bundy and his family spent six summers sailing the lakes on this vessel. But by 1889 the number of the captain's missions had grown to the point that he could not visit them all in one season or even in two seasons in a sailing ship.[23] Bundy needed a steamship.

Bundy once again tapped the resources of his Christian supporters to build his steamship. These included the Newbury family of Detroit and United States Senator McMillan, who together donated $2,500. The fourth *Glad Tidings* cost over $10,000. She was 80 feet long, 18 feet wide and ten feet deep. The new ship had a high pressure engine which carried 140 pounds of steam and could travel through the water at 12 miles an hour. She also had two masts and was schooner rigged. The cabin housed a chapel with a seating capacity of 45 persons. There were also two state rooms, a dining room and a kitchen. Captain Bundy's wife Margaret served as the ship's cook while his 17 year old daughter Agnes played the organ and led the singing.[24]

20 "Capt. Bundy Heard From" *The Chicago Tribune,* September 12, 1879, Page 11
21 "Kenosha Gossip" *The Chicago Tribune,* June 19, 1887, Page 11
22 "Bundy and His Boat" *The Chicago Tribune,* June 11, 1883, Page 7
23 "The Glad Tidings" *The Grand Traverse Herald,* Traverse City, Michigan, June 27, 1889, Page 2
24 *The Grand Traverse Herald,* June 27, 1889, Page 2

Captain Bundy's Glad Tidings docked in Manistique harbor. Photo courtesy Great Lakes Marine Collection of the Milwaukee Public Library/Milwaukee Public Library.

The Gospel steamer was launched from the Miller Brothers' Shipyard in Chicago on June 22, 1889 with a crowd of 8000 people witnessing the event. Agnes Bundy broke a bottle of "eau de cologne" on the ship's bow in place of wine. The new ship was christened the *Glad Tidings*.[25]

Before Bundy could take the newest *Glad Tidings* on its maiden missionary cruise, he had to pass an examination to obtain his steamboat captain's license. He also vowed to find a Christian engineer. The latter proved to be a daunting task.

During the first week in July, Captain Bundy went on an excursion on the steamer *R. J. Gordon* where he interviewed the second engineer. The applicant's discussion with the captain was going well and Bundy had all but hired him to become the engineer on the *Glad Tidings*. The candidate was explaining how much help he would be during the Gospel meetings when something suddenly went awry in the engine room of the *Gordon*. In the feverishness of the moment, the second engineer expressed himself in the off-color language that was common on some secular vessels. Bundy decided that he hadn't yet found the right engineer for his Gospel ship.[26]

The captain was overjoyed with his new steamer as he could visit many more communities during each season. He became known for announcing his arrival at isolated villages with lengthy "howls" from his steam

---

25 "The Glad Tidings is Afloat" *The Chicago Tribune,* June 23, 1889, Page 14
26 "Lake Marine News. Capt. Bundy and His Examination" *The Chicago Tribune,* July 1, 1889, Page 3

whistle.[27] The large onboard chapel assured that he could hold services free of interruptions by unrighteous hecklers. Bundy told reporters: "When the roughs disturb me I take my people aboard my boat and sail away a little ways where we are undisturbed."[28]

The former Gospel Steamer rechristened the Elva. Photo courtesy C. Patrick Labadie Collection/ Thunder Bay National Marine Sanctuary, Alpena, MI.

Tireless in his missionary pursuits, Bundy spent the summer of 1890 on Lakes Michigan and Huron. He averaged over one meeting per day. On the Saginaw River he preached 30 sermons in 20 days.[29]

By 1895 the escalating cost of maintaining the steamer forced the captain to lay up his fourth *Glad Tidings*. The steamer was sold in April of 1896 to a buyer in St. Ignace for $3,900 and was renamed the *Elva*.[30]

From then on, Captain Bundy relied on passenger carriers to continue his work. In 1903, at the age of 77, Bundy was still preaching the Gospel on the street corners. The *Menominee Herald* noted his arrival in the twin cities of Marinette and Menominee in February of that year. He continued preaching until age 79 when poor health compelled him to retire. Bundy's beloved wife Margaret died on January 22, 1904 at the age of 76. The

27 "Overhauling a Gospel Boat" *The Chicago Tribune,* November 21, 1890, Page 6
28 "Glad Tidings By Steam" *The Chicago Tribune,* May 9, 1889, Page 6
29 *The Sentinel,* March 23, 1891, Page 3
30 "Capt. Bundy Sells Out" *The Milwaukee Journal,* Milwaukee, Wisconsin, April 17, 1896, Page 6

captain's life ended two years later on September 15, 1906 at age 80.

Bundy's steamer, *Glad Tidings,* renamed the *Elva,* sailed for several more decades. The *Elva* became part of the Arnold Line ferry fleet. A second deck was added with additional cabins, and the boat was lengthened to 100 feet. The steamer went through several owners and finally in 1944 was converted to a flat top barge to carry supplies to Mackinac Island. The *Elva* was retired in 1952 but that was not the end of the story.

The former Gospel ship was sunk in the Straits of Mackinac on May 12, 1954 in conjunction with the groundbreaking ceremonies for the new Mackinac Bridge.[31] The barge was towed out into the straits between Mackinac Island and St. Ignace. Then it was saturated with oil, loaded with hay and old tires and set ablaze. Fire spread over the deck but the ship stayed afloat, its hull barely visible above the surface of the water. The car ferry *Iroquois* rammed the former Gospel ship with her bow, but the *Elva's* wooden hull remained intact. Lines were attached to the steel ribbing of the ship in an attempt to capsize the boat, but this too was unsuccessful. The coast guard made dozens of high speed passes near the *Elva* which rocked violently back and forth but remained upright. Finally, tons of water were poured into the ship's hold sending the former *Glad Tidings* to the bottom.[32]

The days of schooners, steamboats and seafaring missionaries are past but Captain Bundy and his Gospel ships live on as Great Lakes legend.

---

31 "Straits Bridge Ground-Braking Is Slated This Week End" *Ironwood Daily Globe,* Ironwood, Michigan, May 4, 1954, Page 1

32 "Glad Tidings A Tough Boat" *The Evening News,* Sault Ste. Marie, May 12, 1954, Page 1

Chapter Three:
The Legend of the Christmas Tree Ship

In November of 1912 the three-masted schooner, *Rouse Simmons*, vanished on Lake Michigan. The story of her final voyage has long been shrouded in mystery and conjecture. The schooner was once the pride of the Hackley Lumber Company of Muskegon. But when the aged *Simmons* made her final voyage, she carried a cargo of Christmas trees. The ship set sail from Thompson, Michigan, bound for Chicago just as a powerful November gale swept over the lake. The doomed *Simmons*, along with her captain and crew, never arrived at any port. And the legend began.

Hermann Schuenemann was born in May 1865 in Ahnapee (now Algoma), Wisconsin—the son of German immigrants.[1] He married Barbara Schindel in April of 1891 in Chicago.[2] A daughter Elsie was born one year later. Twin daughters Hazel and Pearl arrived in October of 1898.

Hermann's father, Frederick Schuenemann, was a farmer who made his livelihood from the fertile Wisconsin soil.[3] But Hermann and his older brother August were drawn to the open waters of Lake Michigan. August Schuenemann left the farm at an early age and worked as a sailor out of the port at Ahnapee. After several seasons on the lakes he became part owner of a vessel which he sailed as captain. When Hermann's time came, he charted the same course.[4]

By the 1890s wind powered schooners had grown obsolete as more goods were transported by steamships and railroad cars. Aging sailing ships could be purchased at rock-bottom prices. Their captains sailed from port to port offering to carry whatever merchandise was available. These short-haul mariners and their aging ships filled a vital niche in great lakes commerce.

1   1870 United States Census, Ahnapee, Kewaunee County Wisconsin - Household number 69
2   Marriage License, State of Illinois, Cook County, April 9, 1891
3   Fred Neuschel, *Lives & Legends of the Christmas Tree Ships,* (Ann Arbor: The University of Michigan Press, 2007) 53-54
4   Neuschel, 90

The annual Christmas tree trade in November, near the end of the shipping season, was a risky but lucrative enterprise. The trees had to be brought to market at precisely the right time to maximize profit which meant transporting them in the most dangerous month of the year for sailing. If the trees were brought for sale after the market was saturated prices would drop. Several Lake Michigan captains engaged in the business. Stiff competition was also provided by entrepreneurs who delivered their evergreens by rail.[5]

August Schuenemann was among the first to bring Christmas trees and evergreens to the Chicago Market.[6] He brought three or four vessels filled with trees each holiday season.[7] Schuenemann was only 24 years old in 1875 when he obtained part interest in the aged and dilapidated schooner, *William H. Hinsdale*. This craft likely served as Schuenemann's first Christmas tree ship. The vessel had suffered from severe neglect rendering it nearly unseaworthy. During Schuenemann's ownership, the schooner was involved in several collisions due to problems with the rudder, and on another occasion it nearly sank after becoming waterlogged.[8] The *Hinsdale* was the first in a series of such vessels owned by August Schuenemann throughout his sailing career. Usual cargoes during the shipping season included loads of stone, posts, railroad ties and lumber.

The Christmas tree venture was a perfect fit for the Schuenemann brothers. They had both moved to Chicago and lived in the city's thriving German enclave with its yuletide tradition of the "tannenbaum." August Schuenemann was proficient in the art of sailing and maintaining aging vessels while Hermann (who was 12 years younger) had a more engaging personality and a natural gift for marketing. Together, they more than held their own against the competition.

But tragedy struck in 1898. In September of that year, August Schuenemann purchased the two-masted schooner, *S. Thal*, in Milwaukee for 650 dollars.[9] The 32-ton *Thal* measured 75 feet in length with a 20 foot beam. The vessel was 31 years old, poorly maintained and unsafe to sail. Just six weeks later, on November 9, 1898 Schuenemann commanded the *Thal* on its return voyage from Northeastern Wisconsin as a late autumn storm raced across the lake. Winds ranged from 40-60 miles per

---

5   *The Chicago Daily Inter Ocean,* Chicago, Illinois, December 24, 1887
6   *The Chicago Daily Inter Ocean,* December 24, 1887
7   *The Chicago Daily Inter Ocean,* December 24, 1887
8   Neuschel, *Lives & Legends,* 90 and 229.
9   *The Chicago Daily Tribune,* November 12, 1898

hour as the *Thal* approached the city. Near Glencoe, Illinois a sandbar juts out far into the lake causing the waves to break violently near the coast. Witnesses observed the *Thal* struggle valiantly against the waves to remain in deeper water. She flew a flag at half mast which indicated the vessel was in distress. The *Thal* dropped anchor with its "nose against the gale" in an effort to ride out the storm while the crew manned the bilge pumps.[10] After being anchored for two hours, the sailors made preparations to get underway again. Just as the *Thal* started for home, a heavy gust tore the front foresail to shreds. The *Thal* was spun around toward the treacherous coast. The schooner's cannon fired twice to alert those on shore that the ship was in peril. Then the boat disappeared in the fog. Sometime after dark, the *Thal* struck the sandbar and broke apart. August Schuenemann and his crew of five perished. Though no one saw the ship go down, the debris-strewn coast bore witness to what had occurred. The rocky shore along Glencoe, Illinois, was littered with rotting timbers, seamen's chests, shattered masts, and Christmas trees.[11] The tragedy would have been compounded had not Hermann remained at home to help care for his wife and their newborn twin girls.[12]

Captain Hermann Schuenemann (center) with L. Vandaman (left) and Mr. Colberg (right). Chicago Historical Society Photo DN 0006926

Grief stricken, but resolved to support his family and carry on his brother's legacy, Hermann mustered the courage to sail out on the lake. Within a few short weeks his schooner, the *Mary Collins,* was tied up at

10 *The Chicago Daily Tribune,* November 11, 1898
11 *The Chicago Daily Tribune,* November 11, 1898
12 Rochelle Pennington, *The Historic Christmas Tree Ship* (Pathways Press, 2004) 15

the dock near the Clark Street Bridge loaded with Christmas trees from the forests of Northeastern Wisconsin.[13]

In the years following his brother's death Schuenemann established the Northern Michigan Evergreen Company.[14] He purchased some cutover forest acreage near Thompson in Michigan's Upper Peninsula and harvested the second growth balsam, spruce and pine trees to supply his annual Christmas tree enterprise. He purchased additional trees from local suppliers and had them bundled and shipped by rail to the Thompson pier. Schuenemann also took on a new partner, Captain Charles Nelson. Nelson was an experienced skipper who commanded vessels on the world's oceans before spending the final decades of his career on the Great Lakes.[15]

The *Rouse Simmons* (left) docked at Thompson Harbor.
Photo courtesy Thompson Michigan Historical Group

Schuenemann used a number of schooners during the first decade of the twentieth century as Christmas tree ships. These included the *Mary Collins, Truman Moss* and *George Wrenn*. Any misjudgment while sailing these worn out schooners could bring calamity. In 1900, Schuenemann's *Mary Collins* was lost near Little Harbor, Michigan, a mile west of Thompson. The pilot mistook a kerosene lamp in a remote log cabin for the light at the south dock in Thompson. The *Collins* was wrecked after it ran aground on the limestone shore but the captain and crew were unharmed.[16]

13 Neuschel, 232
14 Neuschel, 6-7
15 Neuschel, 204
16 Roy L. Dodge, *Michigan Ghost Towns, Volume III Upper Peninsula* (Tawas City, Mich.: Glendon Publishing, 1973) 294

Schuenemann's last Christmas tree ship was the *Rouse Simmons*. The three-masted, 220 ton schooner was launched in August of 1868 from the Allan, McClelland & Company Shipyard in Milwaukee. The ships' dimensions were 127 feet in length with a 27 foot beam and the depth of her hold measured 8.4 feet. For 26 years the *Simmons* had been the premier schooner of the shipping fleet of Muskegon lumber baron Charles Hackley. The *Simmons* then passed through a series of owners before it was purchased by Mannes Bonner from St. James, Michigan on Beaver Island. Bonner used the boat locally to transport wood and bark.

The *Simmons* was well past her prime when Captain Schuenemann and his partner, Charles Nelson, became part owners with Bonner in 1910. Captain Nelson had the boat re-caulked and in November of 1911 the *Simmons* replaced the *Wrenn* as Chicago's Christmas tree ship.[17]

On Friday, November 22, 1912 the *Simmons* was tied up at the dock in Thompson, Michigan, as a cargo of Christmas trees was brought aboard. The day had started out unusually mild, with temperatures in the middle 40s. But the mercury crept lower as the day wore on and ominous gray clouds gathered in the western sky. The innocuous weather forecast for the Upper Lakes called for moderate west winds with generally fair weather Friday night and Saturday.[18] As the storm clouds thickened, the captain's friends in Thompson tried in vain to convince him to delay his departure, or to have his evergreens delivered by rail instead. John Hruska, who owned the meat market, warned him not to go.[19] So did saloon owner Simon Bouschor. He noticed that his barometer had fallen dramatically and was headed even lower.[20] But Captain Schuenemann's mind was made up. He wanted to set sail just as soon as his schooner was fully loaded. He knew the children back home waited for their Christmas trees.

Schuenemann had several reasons for wanting to set sail from Thompson. He sought to dominate the Christmas tree market and timing was crucial. He may have feared that if he postponed his departure he could be delayed for several days or even weeks, especially if winter arrived early. A master of publicity and marketing, Schuenemann had painstakingly established his reputation as Chicago's "Captain Santa." Selling his trees from the decks of schooners docked at the center of commerce near Chicago's

---

17 Neuschel, 205
18 *The Evening News,* Sault Ste. Marie, November 22, 1912
19 Pennington, 169-171
20 Dodge, 295. See also, Jack Orr, *Lumberjacks and River Pearls* (Manistique, Michigan: Pioneer Tribune, Dec. 1979) 17.

Clark Street Bridge had been his innovation. Finally, Schuenemann was a philanthropist of sorts. Raised in poverty due his father's illness, he had a special affection for children and provided Christmas trees free of charge to poor families and orphanages.

The hold of the aged ship brimmed with evergreens, and the remainder would be piled on the deck. The tightly bundled trees were stacked 10 to 12 feet high, covered over with green shiplap boards and tied down securely.[21] The booms of the sails were raised to accommodate the load. If Schuenemann could get his cargo to Chicago by Thanksgiving, the profits would be substantial.

As more and more trees were brought aboard some of the crew became anxious. Several witnesses, both in Chicago and in Thompson, observed rats scurry from the ship which was a particularly bad omen among sailors. Captains Nelson and Schuenemann were seen onboard engaged in a heated discussion. At least one crew member, Hogan Hoganson, thought the ship was overloaded and refused to sail on the *Simmons*. He forfeited his pay and took a train back to Chicago, instead.[22]

The *Simmons* was fully loaded by late afternoon and was towed out of Thompson harbor at dusk. Captain Schuenemann reasoned that the strong northwest wind would speed the arrival of the *Simmons* home. Captain August Hansen piloted another schooner, the *Butcher Boy,* toward the safe harbor at nearby Manistique. He couldn't believe his eyes when he caught sight of the *Simmons*. "I said to the others, 'Captain Schuenemann must be in a terrible hurry to get those trees to market. I wouldn't go out into this storm for all the trees the [ocean liner] *Maretania* could carry. Those boys will be lucky if they don't go to the bottom.'"[23]

By the morning of November 23, conditions on the lake had deteriorated dramatically. The sailors aboard the *Simmons* battled for their survival against the full fury of the storm. Although the temperature remained above freezing, hypothermia was a real threat. Enormous waves washed over the deck and gale force winds battered the sails. Water seeped into the hold from around the hatch covers which added even more weight to the ship. Captain Charles Nelson, the more experienced skipper, was at the helm and struggled to keep the *Simmons* on course and afloat. Nelson was 69 years old and retired. He had reluctantly come along after Captain

---

21 Neuschel, 7 and Orr, 17. See also *Chicago Daily News*, December 5, 1912
22 *Chicago Inter Ocean,* December 5, 1912 See also *Chicago Record-Herald,* Dec. 5, 1912
23 *The Sheboygan Press,* December 19, 1912

Schuenemann pleaded with him to take command on this final voyage of the year.²⁴ The decision would cost Nelson his life.

At 2:00 p.m. on Saturday, November 23, the *Ann Arbor No. 5* car ferry steamed out of the harbor at Manitowoc, Wisconsin, bound for Frankfort, Michigan. After the captain of the car ferry discovered just how turbulent the lake had become, he aborted his plans and headed north for the safety of the Sturgeon Bay Ship Canal. The steamer was sailing several miles north of Kewaunee and about five miles off shore when the captain spotted an unidentified three-masted schooner a half-mile away heading south. The ship's mainsail was down and was using only its short sails for propulsion. The vessel was heeled over in the wind and laboring but was not flying any distress signals. The car ferry captain steered a course clear of the schooner, thinking surely that the old ship would find shelter in a nearby harbor.²⁵

Ann Arbor No. 5 (right) docked in Green Bay.
Schoolcraft County Historical Society photo, Niles/Helmka Family Collection

About one hour later the watchman at the Kewaunee Lifesaving Station spotted a three-masted schooner headed south well off shore with distress flags flying. The life station's captain was notified but decided not to send his row boat to the schooner's aid in the heavy seas. Instead, the captain attempted to procure a gasoline powered boat but was unsuccessful. Frustrated in his attempts to obtain a suitable craft, the captain called the next lifesaving station to the south where he knew a gasoline powered lifeboat was available.²⁶

24 *Chicago Daily News,* December 5, 1912
25 *Sturgeon Bay Advocate,* January 23, 1913
26 Neuschel, 14-15

Captain Sogge of the Two Rivers Lifesaving Station took the call from Captain Craite at 3:10 p.m. Ten minutes later he and his crew launched their lifeboat and headed north against a strong northwest wind. Despite the rough waters and near freezing temperatures, visibility on the lake was excellent. By 6:30 p.m. the lifesavers had traveled 13 miles north toward Kewaunee and hadn't seen any sign of the schooner. At this point, a heavy snow commenced which dramatically decreased visibility. A disappointed and perplexed Captain Sogge headed back toward Two Rivers with his crew.[27]

Two other ships were lost on Lake Michigan and one on Lake Superior during the same storm —all in sight of witnesses. The fishing tug *Two Brothers*, with a crew of three perished near Pentwater, Michigan; the schooner *Three Sisters* foundered in Green Bay with no survivors; and on Lake Superior, the passenger ferry *South Shore* became another grim statistic.

Back in Chicago, friends and relatives of the crew of the *Rouse Simmons* waited for the ship to arrive. Each morning was filled with anticipation but was rewarded only with disappointment. Their alarm increased with each day that passed. When the *Simmons* hadn't come into port by November 28, which was Thanksgiving Day, the families demanded action. They notified government officials that the *Simmons* was overdue. Lifesaving stations around the lake were contacted for any news of the Christmas ship. Perhaps the *Simmons* had found safe harbor in some remote port and was merely delayed. However, other than the sightings of an unidentified three-masted schooner by the *Ann Arbor No. 5* and the watchman at the Kewaunee Lifesaving Station, there was nothing to be learned. The fate of the *Rouse Simmons* was unknown.

Captain Berry of the revenue cutter Tuscarora was ordered by the Treasury Secretary in Washington to conduct a search for the *Simmons*.[28] On December 4, 1912, the captain went through the motions. The Tuscarora's cruise was conducted primarily in the fog in the waters between Two Rivers, Wisconsin and Waukegan, Illinois, well south of where the Christmas ship was last sighted. Not surprisingly, no trace of the *Simmons* was found.

---

27 Neuschel, 14-15
28 *Duluth News Tribune,* Dec. 6, 1912

The *Rouse Simmons*; Courtesy the Great Lakes Marine Collection of the Milwaukee Public Library.

Then on December 6, 1912 the Chicago papers reported that all hope for the *Rouse Simmons* had been lost. Christmas trees had washed ashore on the eastern shore of the lake in Pentwater, Michigan. Also on December 6, the *Chicago Daily News* reported large numbers of Christmas trees littered the beach in Sturgeon Bay, Wisconsin. These reports, like many others concerning the *Simmons* proved to be fiction.[29] In truth, debris strewn on the beach in Pentwater (which did not include Christmas trees) was from the sunken fishing tug *Two Brothers* and not the *Simmons*. The *Chicago Daily News* attributed its report of large numbers of Christmas trees coming ashore in Sturgeon Bay to shipbuilder, A. S. Putnam, who the paper claimed had participated in a phone interview with one of their reporters. Newspapers in Sturgeon Bay denied the report, and the Chicago Police Department sent a detective to investigate. The conclusion of the investigation published in the Chicago *Inter Ocean* was that there was no truth to the story that Christmas trees and wreckage from the *Rouse Simmons* had washed ashore in Sturgeon Bay.[30]

Captain Sogge of the Two Rivers Lifesaving Station read the papers too. He decided to satisfy his own curiosity regarding the fate of the *Simmons*. On December 6, 1912, he made a thorough search of the lakeshore between

---

29 Neuschel, 199. See also, *Chicago Inter Ocean,* Dec. 12, 1912
30 Neuschel, *Lives and Legends,* 190-191

Two Rivers and Kewaunee for any sign of wreckage. Sogge launched his lifeboat at 8:00 a.m. and traveled north for 18 miles along the shore. He reported "not a particle" of debris was found.[31]

Then on December 13, 1912, the *Chicago American* reported an astonishing find. A fisherman from Sheboygan, Wisconsin had spotted a bottle bobbing in the water. It was sealed with a wooden stopper, presumably whittled from the limb of a Christmas tree. Inside the bottle was a "penciled note in faltering hand" from the captain of the *Rouse Simmons*. "Friday—Everybody goodbye. I guess we are all through. Sea washed over our deckload on Thursday. During the night the small boat was washed off. Leaking badly. Engwald and Steve fell overboard Thursday. God help us. Herman Schuenemann."

Speculation abounded about the message in the bottle. There were obvious errors in the note. The *Simmons* had spent Thursday, November 21 at the dock in Thompson, Michigan. It departed the harbor at dusk on Friday evening and was seen by the captain of the *Ann Arbor No. 5* and the lookout at the Kewaunee Lifesaving Station in the early afternoon on Saturday. But sailors argued that a man about to lose his life on a sinking ship might easily be confused about the day of the week.

Relatives were desperate for any scrap of credible information. The mother of Philip Bausewein, one of the crew members on the *Simmons*, wrote the Sheboygan Police Department requesting that the letter found in the bottle be turned over to the family. The police department responded that the report was false and that no such letter was found. The man who had allegedly discovered the note was unknown among fisherman in the area.[32] The cruel hoax was just another invention of the Chicago newspapers.

With the fate of the Christmas ship still in doubt, the Treasury Secretary ordered the revenue cutter *Mackinac*, based in Sault Ste. Marie, to make a thorough search of the widely scattered islands along the northern shore of Lake Michigan. Perhaps the *Simmons* sought shelter from the storm in some isolated harbor and was stranded. She may have run aground or become trapped in the ice. The search began on December 15, 1912. A stop was made at St James, Michigan on Beaver Island, where the majority owner of the *Rouse Simmons,* Captain Mannes Bonner, came aboard to assist. Captain Bonner reported that contact had already been

---

31 Neuschel, 192
32 *The Sheboygan Press,* Dec. 20, 1912

made with many of the islands.³³ The mission was abandoned two days later on December 17, 1912.³⁴

Friends in the maritime community rallied around the families. The *Chicago Inter Ocean* newspaper established a fund to aid all the families of the men lost on the *Rouse Simmons*. The exact number of crewman and anonymous timber cutters who hitched a ride on the *Simmons* during her final voyage will never be known. Estimates ranged from 11 to 18 men.

Hermann Schuenemann's widow, Barbara and his oldest daughter Elsie were determined to carry on despite their loss. Two railroad cars loaded with excess Christmas trees sent by Captain Schuenemann arrived from Upper Michigan. The W. C. Holmes Shipping Company loaned the schooner *Oneida* to the Schuenemann family for use as a Christmas tree ship.³⁵ The schooner was docked near the Clark Street Bridge and volunteers filled its deck with Christmas trees. Barbara and Elsie busily fashioned garlands and wreaths from evergreen boughs. The yuletide tradition continued each year until the death of Barbara Schuenemann in 1933.

By January of 1913 the fate of the Christmas tree ship had faded from the headlines. Nearly everyone concluded that the *Simmons* became waterlogged in the storm and sank with all onboard.

Unbelievably, on July 31, 1913, news of the *Simmons* again appeared on the front pages. *The Sturgeon Bay Advocate* reported that another bottle containing a message from the doomed crew had washed up on the beach. It was found by a boy near Whitefish Bay. The note was purportedly written by Captain Charles Nelson. "November 23, 1912. These lines were written at 10:30 p.m. Schooner Rouse Simmons ready to go down about 20 miles southwest of Two Rivers Point, between 15 and 20 miles offshore. All hands lashed to one line. Goodbye. Capt. Charles Nelson." This second message in a bottle was widely reported but future evidence regarding the actual location of the *Simmons* shipwreck would reveal it was also a hoax.

Eleven years later, in April of 1924 the fishing tug *Reindeer* brought up its nets a short distance off Two Rivers, Wisconsin. The nets were brought ashore and dumped on the beach to dry. Lighthouse keeper Henry Gattie was present and discovered an object ensnared in the mesh. It was a

---

33 Neuschel, 199
34 *The Evening News,* Sault Ste. Marie, Michigan, Dec. 17, 1912
35 Pennington, 256. See also, Neuschel, 206

burgundy wallet, wrapped in oil skin and tied with a heavy cord or rubber band. Inside the billfold—perfectly preserved—was the personal business card of Captain Hermann Schuenemann. Other items included newspaper clippings from Manistique, Michigan along with expense receipts for the purchase of Christmas trees and other provisions dated November, 1912.[36] The wallet and its contents were delivered to the Schuenemann family. The discovery of the captain's billfold provided circumstantial evidence that the *Simmons* had gone down near where she was last seen, between Kewaunee and Two Rivers, Wisconsin.

It would be another 47 years before the shipwreck was located. On October 30, 1971, Milwaukee scuba diver Kent Bellrichard crisscrossed the choppy waters north of Two Rivers, Wisconsin with a borrowed boat and sonar equipment. Bellrichard's trained ear recognized when the sonar detected a large object on the bottom of the lake. After pinpointing the exact location, Bellrichard put on his scuba equipment and dove down to investigate. Lying on the bottom in 165 feet of water was a three-masted schooner. The vessel was completely intact and in remarkably good condition. Visibility was an issue as Bellrichard's light was only capable of illuminating a distance of 10 or 12 feet, and at some point during his dive the light went out. As he ascended to his boat, an excited Bellrichard was sure he had discovered the wreck of the Christmas tree ship but proof would be established on future dives.[37]

The evidence would be irrefutable. Clearly visible on the side of the sunken craft was the name *Rouse Simmons* and skeletons of Christmas trees filled her hold. Several artifacts were recovered from the *Simmons*. These included a wooden stool, an enamel kettle and a piece of china with the initials R. S. The largest artifact recovered was the anchor which weighed one ton and was raised in 1973.[38]

The story of the Christmas Ship has endured for nearly a century, due in part to the personality of her captain and the perseverance of the Schuenemann family in the face of overwhelming loss. Captain Schuenemann sold thousands of Christmas trees each year, with the finest trees going to some of the most prominent businesses in the city.

---

36 *Sheboygan Press-Telegram,* Sheboygan, Wisconsin, April 4, 1924. See also, *Manitowoc Herald-Times,* Manitowoc, Wisconsin, Dec. 6, 1971
37 Pennington, 232-234. See also, *Manitowoc Herald-Times,* Dec. 6, 1971
38 Pennington, 235. See also, *The Sheboygan Press,* June 5, 1974

Schuenemann (nicknamed Captain Santa) was much beloved in Chicago. He became known for his cheerful disposition and his many acts of kindness. Every holiday season Schuenemann presented gifts of Christmas trees, wreaths and garlands to both local churches and the Orphans home. Trees were also given away to poor families. The whole endeavor was a family affair with the captain's wife and daughters helping out. After the captain's death, his family carried on the tradition for another 20 years. Trees were shipped by rail from Upper Michigan and sold from the decks of rented schooners. Sometime later, the business was moved to a store front near the Clark Street Bridge where the Christmas ships once docked.

Despite his tremendous success, Captain Schuenemann was not a rich man. The Christmas tree business was run on a shoestring budget. A leaden sky, a strong northwest wind and a dramatic drop in the barometric pressure foretold disaster. But Captain Schuenemann gambled everything to get his evergreens to market by Thanksgiving. The children were waiting for their Christmas trees. So, the *Rouse Simmons* sailed out of Thompson harbor and disappeared into oblivion. In Chicago, the children waited.

With an absence of information, unscrupulous journalists made up stories, and pranksters perpetrated hoaxes. Myths were intertwined with facts—and a legend was born.

Chapter Four:
The Lumberman's Daughter

Headlines on the front pages of leading Wisconsin newspapers proclaimed "A Romantic Affair." The daughter of a wealthy Upper Michigan lumberman had eloped with her first cousin, a charming professional singer from Oshkosh, Wisconsin. Convinced her young man was a rogue, the lumberman was livid. The newspapers portrayed the rich father as a cynical tycoon who valued wealth and status more than his daughter's happiness. The newspapers had it wrong.

Constant (Con) Ruggles was born in Naples, Maine on March 28, 1842, the son of Daniel and Abigail (Foster) Ruggles.[1] The family migrated west to Oshkosh, Wisconsin where in August of 1860, Ruggles married Augusta Scott. This union would produce four children: Abbie, Harry, Reginald and Maud.

Following the outbreak of the Civil War, Ruggles enlisted in the Union army. He was mustered into service as a private in the 58th Illinois Infantry on November 1, 1861. Army records document that he stood five feet, five inches tall with blonde hair, a fair complexion and grey eyes.

In February of 1862, the 58th was encamped in front of Fort Donelson on the Cumberland River in western Tennessee. The men slept on the ground for four days without benefit of shelter or camp fires. The strenuous duty and exposure to the elements took a toll on Ruggles' health. He spent several months in the hospital and was discharged due to disability in September of 1862. After his discharge, he returned to Oshkosh where he regained his health and pursued a career in the lumber industry.

Con Ruggles and his family moved to Manistique, on the northern shore of Lake Michigan in November of 1875. Ruggles had invested in virgin pine timberland north of Thunder Lake in Schoolcraft County. He partnered

---
1   National Archives Civil War Pension File, Constant M. Ruggles, General Affidavit dated May 6, 1913.

with Ebenezer and William James in the James Brothers' sawmill. The business thrived for several years until a forest fire nearly destroyed the enterprise. The flames consumed a large quantity of lumber, a barn, ice house and a half mile of railroad track used to transport the lumber to the harbor.[2] But Ruggles had diverse business interests including a butcher shop, strawberry farm, livery stable, and a stage coach line. He also was the proprietor of Manistique's premier hotel, the Ossawinamakee. With the death of his father in 1888, the lumberman inherited even more money.[3] By 1890 he had amassed a sizable fortune.

During the summer of 1890, Eugene Robbins came to Upper Michigan to visit his mother's relatives. Robbins' uncle, Fred Scott, lived in Thompson and his aunt Augusta Scott Ruggles lived in nearby Manistique. The 22 year old Robbins was instantly attracted to the Ruggles' youngest daughter Maud. She was a beautiful 16 year old brunette with a sweet singing voice. A romance blossomed. Robbins sung professionally in Oshkosh and he encouraged Maud to develop her singing skills. The two became inseparable. When Robbins proposed marriage, Maud accepted. However, her parents vehemently opposed the match and forbade Maud from continuing the relationship. Robbins returned to Oshkosh alone.

The following winter Maud Ruggles traveled to Oshkosh to study music. She stayed in the home of her older sister, Abbie Brundage. Within a few weeks, the romance with her talented cousin was rekindled. Robbins entertained regularly at local social functions. Now, he was joined in the spotlight by his cousin Maud. They sang a duet at a G.A.R. campfire in February of 1891 and performed solos the following month at a concert in Oshkosh.[4]

A ROMANTIC AFFAIR.

The Elopement of Miss Ruggles, of Manistique, and Gene Robbins, of Oshkosh.

OSHKOSH, Wis., May 20. —The elopement to Winneconne of Eugene Robbins, of this city, and Miss Maud Ruggles, of Manistique, Mich., was one of the most romantic affairs which has occurred in this county for many years. The bride, who is a cousin of the groom, is a daughter of Mr. Con. Ruggles, the Manistique lumberman. The latter and his wife are said to be highly incensed over the marriage. A telegram was sent to Mr. Ruggles after his daughter disappeared and, he is expected to be in Oshkosh today.

So, it came as no surprise when the pair eloped to nearby Winneconne

---

2   "Fire at Monastique," *Oshkosh Daily Northwestern*, Oshkosh, Wisconsin, August 7, 1878.
3   Manistee County Probate Court Archives, Estate of Daniel D. Ruggles, Last Will and Testament dated August 4, 1885.
4   "Camp Fire and Dance," *Oshkosh Daily Northwestern*, February 20, 1891 page 4. See also: "The Old Boys in Blue," *The Sunday Sentinel*, Milwaukee, Wisconsin, March 1, 1891, page 1

in May of 1891 and were married by a Justice of the Peace.[5] Rumors spread in the press that Con Ruggles was angry with his daughter and had disowned her. Maud wrote a letter to her father and begged his forgiveness—but the envelope was returned unopened.[6]

The couple would have to make a living without the support of Maud's wealthy parents. Robbins was employed as a painter but dreamed of a full-time career as a professional singer. He persuaded Maud to join him on the stage with the James Browne Theatre Company of Chicago. The contract was signed in June of 1891. They would receive a joint salary of $15.00 per week.[7]

The Browne Theatre Company consisted of 23 artists, including actors and musicians.[8] The troupe performed at opera houses throughout Wisconsin and Michigan. Admission prices ranged from 15 to 35 cents. Plays included the comedies, *A Waif of the Sea, Chain Lightning,* and *The Girl I Love.* The five-act drama *Myrtle Ferns* was also on the playbill. Between acts and during scene changes, the audience was entertained by "beautiful songs sung by first class artists."

The Robbins duo was an immediate hit with theater goers. The publicity created by their elopement and the subsequent rift with Mrs. Robbins' father drew curious spectators to the opera houses. The reviews were glowing. The *Ironwood Advocate* proclaimed that "Mr. and Mrs. Robbins are without doubt, two of the finest singers who have ever appeared in this city."[9] In Ashland, Wisconsin the critic noted that the solo by Mrs. E. P. Robbins was "sweetly rendered" and the audience demanded an encore.[10]

Despite the public impression that the newlyweds had found happiness on the stage, in reality, their marital relationship had already started to unravel. Robbins would frequently leave the theater after the evening's performance and spend the remainder of the night with a deck of poker cards and a bottle of liquor. Maud was left alone in their hotel room.

Fortunately, Maud's relationship with her family had improved. She was

---

5   "Wedded at Winneconne," *Oshkosh Daily Northwestern,* May 19, 1891, See also, "A Romantic Affair," *The Milwaukee Journal,* Milwaukee, Wisconsin, May 20, 1891, page 1.
6   "Going On The Stage," *Oshkosh Daily Northwestern,* June 29, 1891, page 1.
7   Schoolcraft County Michigan Circuit Court Archives, "Bill of Complaint," Maud Ruggles Robbins vs. Eugene Robbins, February 4, 1893.
8   *Ironwood Advocate,* Ironwood, Michigan, January 25, 1892, page 4.
9   "Local Laconics" *Ironwood Advocate,* Ironwood, Michigan, January 26, 1892.
10 "The Opera House Crowded" *Gogebic Iron Spirit,* Bessemer, Michigan, January 16, 1892, p.1.

warmly received at her parental home but her husband wasn't permitted to pass over the threshold. Despite Maud's disappointment in Robbins' drinking and gambling, she defended him against all criticism. Her parents occasionally sent her money which Maud gratefully accepted.[11] All of her theater earnings were squandered by Eugene Robbins on booze and gambling debts.[12]

In January of 1892, the Browne Theatre Company visited Manistique. Carey W. Dunton, a lawyer and personal friend of the Ruggles family, was asleep in his room on the third floor of the Ossawinamakee Hotel. He was awakened at 3:00 a.m. by someone noisily ascending the stairway. Dunton went to the door to check out the disturbance. He immediately recognized an intoxicated Eugene Robbins being assisted up the stairs by hotel staff. Robbins was brought to his room which was near Dunton's. After Robbins disappeared into his room, the young lawyer heard noises, muffled voices and then all was quiet except the sound of a woman weeping.[13]

The Ossawinamakee Hotel. Photo Courtesy Schoolcraft County Historical Society.

In mid-April of 1892, the theater troupe appeared at Port Huron, Michigan. One late afternoon a drunken Eugene Robbins arrived back at

11 Schoolcraft County Curcuit Court archives, "Affidavits of Constant M. Ruggles and Augusta Ruggles," Maud Ruggles Robbins vs. Eugene Robbins, November 3, 1893.
12 Schoolcraft County Circuit Court archives, "Bill of Complaint," Maud Ruggles Robbins vs. Eugene Robbins, February 4, 1893.
13 Schoolcraft County Circuit Court archives, " Affidavit of Carey W. Dunton," Maud Ruggles Robbins vs. Eugene Robbins, November 3, 1893.

the hotel prior to the evening's performance. Troupe manager Browne was concerned that Robbins would be unable to entertain as scheduled. Charles McCallum and five of his sisters, all from Cheboygan, were musicians with the company. The manager asked McCallum to take Robbins [14] outside and walk with him in the evening air. McCallum did his best but when they returned Robbins was still too impaired to go on stage.

The following day McCallum's sister Frankie noticed that Maud had not come down to the dining room for breakfast or lunch. Frankie's instincts told her something was wrong. She went to Maud's room and found the young singer alone and in tears. Her face and arms were bruised and swollen. Maud confided to Frankie that her husband had abused her.[15] The previous evening an enraged Robbins had thrown Maud around the room and struck her repeatedly.[16]

Maud was disconsolate and confused. She convinced herself that if she tried harder to please her husband, his drinking and abuse would cease—but instead, he became even more callous.

By May of 1892, Mr. and Mrs. Robbins were no longer employed with the theater troupe. Poor health was the reason given to the newspapers for their return to Oshkosh. But manager Browne likely voided their contract due to Eugene Robbins' habitual drunkenness and numerous missed performances.

On May 20, 1892 Maud and her husband were returning to the residence of Maud's in-laws, Stephen and Hannah Robbins, after a visit to the home of Maud's sister, Abbie Brundage. Without warning, Eugene Robbins reached into his vest pocket and pulled out a pistol. He pointed it at Maud's head and threatened to shoot. Terrified, Maud realized that her husband might eventually kill her. Robbins returned the revolver to his pocket, having delivered the message that he was still in control.[17]

By June, the couple had moved into a place of their own. Eugene Robbins' abuse of alcohol continued unabated. One night in mid-June a drunken Robbins assaulted Maud and inflicted injuries.[18] A few days later Maud visited her sister, who was alarmed when she saw Maud's swollen,

14 Schoolcraft County Circuit Court archives. "Affidavit of Frankie McCallum." Maud Ruggles Robbins vs. Eugene Robbins, November 3, 1893.
15 Ibid.
16 Schoolcraft County Michigan Circuit Court Archives, "Bill of Complaint," Maud Ruggles Robbins vs. Eugene Robbins, February 4, 1893.
17 Ibid.
18 Ibid.

bruised and bloodshot eye. Abbie suspected that her sister was being physically abused but Maud denied it.[19] She insisted that the injury was accidental. The conversation eventually turned to other family matters. Abbie informed Maud that their mother was due to arrive in a few days from Manistique. The visit was expected to last for several weeks.[20] Maud saw her chance and plotted her getaway.

Several days went by without any opportunity for Maud to leave. Then in the early morning hours of June 23, 1892, Eugene Robbins staggered home. He reeked of alcohol and passed out on the bed. At daybreak, Maud slipped out of the house and fled to her sister's. Maud was frantic by the time she arrived at the Brundage home. She demanded to see her mother. Nearly hysterical, Maud explained that she intended to escape from her husband. He was asleep but when he woke up, he would come looking for her. Mrs. Ruggles knew what to do. She hurriedly packed her bags and left immediately with Maud for the railroad station. They took the first train out of town bound for Milwaukee. From there, mother and daughter traveled to the docks and boarded a passenger liner for a leisurely cruise back to Manistique.[21]

Reginald Ruggles (left) and Wm. Kefauver (right) appeared in amateur theatrical performances in Manistique. Pictured above is a scene from the comic opera, The Little Tycoon. Schoolcraft County Historical Society Photo

Eugene Robbins arrived at the Brundage home later that afternoon in search of his wife. He was told that Maud had left for her parent's home in Manistique. Robbins boarded the train the following day for Upper

19 "Home With Father," *Oshkosh Daily Northwestern,* July 15, 1892, p.1.
20 Ibid.
21 Ibid.

Michigan. After he detrained at the depot in Manistique, Robbins sent friends to the Ruggles home to make inquiries. Maud was not there. She and her mother were still on the steamer from Milwaukee.[22]

> **AN OSOKOOH SENSATION.**
>
> Sequel to the Romantic Marriage of Maude Ruggles and Gene Robbins.
>
> OSHKOSH, Wis., July 15.—The sequel to an elopement sensation developed here today. About a year ago Miss Maude Ruggles, daughter C. M. Ruggles, the wealthy lumberman of Manistique, Mich., while here studying music, eloped with Eugene P. Robbins, her cousin and a singer of some note, who was objectionable to Miss Ruggles' parents. Robbins had met his cousin while spending the previous summer in Manistique and the girl's father had, at that time, vetoed the marriage. The young couple, however, were married at some small town in this vicinity and although the bride was welcomed to her home whenever she chose to go, Robbins was never admitted beneath the parental roof.
>
> The young couple went on the stage with the Brown Theatre company and were very successful.
>
> A few weeks ago the wife went home to her father. Robbins gave out that it was only for a visit, and that he would soon join her and the two would go out from Chicago with Daniels Opera Co. in the fall. It now developes through a statement of Mrs. G. H. Brundage, a sister of Mrs. Robbins, that the bride has deserted Robbins and gone home to stay. Robbins is a pleasant fellow and very popular. The affair will stir up a big sensation.

Article from *The Milwaukee Journal*, July 15, 1892, p.1

On July 5, 1892 an item appeared on the front page of the Oshkosh *Daily Northwestern* which announced that Mr. and Mrs. Eugene Robbins had signed a contract to join the Daniels Opera Company of Chicago. The article went on to say that Maud Robbins was visiting friends and relatives in Manistique but would join her husband in two weeks to begin rehearsals in Chicago. The news was quickly denied by members of the Ruggles family who declared that Maud had left her husband and intended to file for divorce.

Soon after the article appeared Eugene Robbins left Oshkosh for Thompson, Michigan, a few miles south of Manistique on Lake Michigan. Robbins stayed with his uncle, Fred Scott, who owned a farm in the area. Robbins hoped to reconcile with Maud. But after two weeks he had only managed a brief meeting during a chance encounter in Manistique.[23]

Near the end of July, Robbins decided to pay Maud a visit at the Ruggles home. Robbins walked from his uncle's farm to Manistique, where he arrived in the late afternoon. He began the four-mile trek to the Ruggles' farm at dusk. Increasing darkness and fog slowed his progress over the trail. He was about two miles from his destination, near a creek-bed, when he was startled by the sound of voices. One of them shouted "Give it to

22 Ibid.
23 "The Story of Robbins," *Oshkosh Daily Northwestern,* August 15, 1892

him." Robbins was attacked by two men. A blow to his jaw spun him around. His hat was jerked down over his face covering his eyes. Robbins absorbed several punches before one of the men pulled out a knife. The blade stung his flesh as it slashed his chest and side and left a deep gash in his arm. Crying out in pain, Robbins collapsed on the ground. His assailants fled. Several minutes passed before the wounded man started back to Manistique where he found lodging in a hotel and received medical attention for his injuries.[24]

Although he made no direct accusations against his brothers-in-law, Harry and Reginald Ruggles, Robbins let it be known that he had received threats from them in the past.[25] The brothers had been in Manistique before Robbins started out to see Maud at the Ruggles' farm. Robbins cast himself as the victim but he merely reaped a portion of what he had sown. No charges were ever filed.

Maud remained in Manistique and resided in her father's home. She filed for a divorce from Eugene Robbins in the Schoolcraft County Circuit Court on February 4, 1893. Maud was only 19 years old and still legally considered an "infant." Her father, Con Ruggles, was appointed by the Court as Maud's "next friend" to represent her in the proceedings. Eugene Robbins was served with a subpoena but did not appear to contest the divorce. Circuit Court Judge Joseph H. Steere issued the divorce decree on November 4, 1893 on the grounds of extreme cruelty.[26]

Eugene Robbins married Gertrude Morrill in 1894 and for a time continued to pursue a career as a professional singer. In the early 1900s he served as a jailer, deputy sheriff and undersheriff in Eau Claire, Wisconsin. He later owned a farm in Augusta, Wisconsin before moving to Minneapolis in 1915 where he was employed with a bank. He moved to California in 1940 and died in Ripon, California in November of 1943 at age 76.[27] It is unknown if he ever conquered his demons.

Maud continued to live with her parents for the next several years. She married Charles McCallum (formerly of the Browne Theatre Company) in Cheboygan, Michigan on June 29, 1907. McCallum's first wife had died and he had a 9 year old son. McCallum's sister Frankie now became

24 Ibid.
25 Ibid.
26 Schoolcraft County Michigan Circuit Court Archives, "Decree For Divorce," Maud Ruggles Robbins vs. Eugene Robbins, November 4, 1893.
27 "Eugene P. Robbins, Former Resident of Oshkosh, Passes Away," *Oshkosh Daily Northwestern,* November 22, 1943, p.4.

Maud's sister-in-law.

Sadly, Maud was denied a long and happy life. Succumbing to cancer, she passed away in Detroit on June 24, 1913 at age 38.[28] Maud's parents accompanied her body on the train back to Oshkosh. Her funeral took place in the home of her sister Abbie Brundage, The former entertainer was buried in the Ruggles family plot in Oshkosh. No longer a romantic sensation, her obituary appeared on page 14 of the local paper.[29]

Con Ruggles moved to the Chicago area in 1898 where he owned a foundry which he operated for several years with his sons Harry and Reginald. He moved to St. Joseph, Michigan in 1909 and became a prominent fruit farmer. His wife of 60 years, Augusta Ruggles, passed away in October of 1920. The aged lumberman died on September 13, 1925 in St. Joseph at age 83.

---

28 State of Michigan, Death Certificate dated June 24, 1913.
29 "Obituary," *Oshkosh Daily Northwestern,* June 27, 1913, p.14.

Chapter Five:
The Downfall of a Dive Keeper

Dan Heffron, Image Courtesy *The Waterloo Courier*, May 4, 1892

For nearly 12 years Dan Heffron had thwarted all attempts to bring him to justice, but his day of reckoning finally came in March of 1892. As the jury in the Upper Peninsula lumbering town of Manistique prepared to enter the courtroom to deliver its guilty verdict, Heffron cheated the law for a final time. Hiding under a buffalo robe, he slipped out of town in a horse drawn sleigh.

Dan Heffron was born in Ontario Canada in 1855, the son of William and Annie Heffron, and the oldest of five brothers including Dennis, Larry, Michael and Thomas.[1] Dan immigrated first to New York before coming to Michigan in the 1870s. According to legend, Dan found work with a lumber company in Cheboygan, Michigan where he systematically stole a portion of his crew's wages. The lumberjacks received their pay in time checks, which Dan discounted from 10 to 20 percent. Before long he had skimmed enough money to invest in even more lucrative albeit illegal enterprises.[2]

Arriving in Manistique in the late 1870s, Dan hoped to enter the saloon business, but he soon discovered that all the property in town was controlled by the Chicago Lumbering Company. The company's owners were temperance men who sought to keep Manistique a dry community. The deeds prohibited use of their property for the sale of alcohol, to wit:

---

1   Wisconsin Death Records, Lawrence Heffron, 1890; See Also, 1871 Canadian Census Records, Humberstone, Welland, Ontario.
2   "A Divekeeper's Wealth," *The Waterloo Courier,* Waterloo, Iowa, May 4, 1892, p.1.

> "It is understood and agreed between the respective parties hereto that all lands herein mentioned shall never be used by the party of the second part, its successors or assigns, for the business of manufacturing, storing or selling intoxicating liquors, whether distilled or fermented, nor for a house or place of prostitution or assignation, nor for any business or occupation prohibited or punished by the law of the land."[3]

By 1880 however, Dan succeeded in opening a bawdy house just outside the Manistique city limits in Hiawatha Township. The 1880 census identifies four boarders at the house, all women whose occupations were recorded as prostitutes.[4] The mortifying presence of a "house of ill fame" soon became a well-known fact in the lumbering community.

Twelve-year-old Dave Byers from Hiawatha Township had an unexpected encounter with Heffron's "boarders" while delivering venison to customers in Manistique.

> "My cousin Mart Byers handed me a quarter of venison to deliver to a large house across the street while he made another delivery. I made the mistake of entering the front door where I found several 'ladies' in loose garments lounging here and there. After I made my exit through the rear door, Mart told me that was the way I should have entered.[5]

Heffron also discovered a prime block of real estate in the shape of a flat iron that was claimed by Alexander Richards and not subject to the legal restrictions imposed by the lumber company. Dan purchased the land and together with his brother Dennis, they built the Arcade Saloon. The tavern's location at the busy intersection of Pearl and Water Streets in Manistique was perfectly situated to entice thirsty laborers going to and from work at the mill.[6] The upper floor of the saloon housed rooms for billiards and gambling, including an area for prize fights. The business prospered and soon expanded to include a livery stable next door.

---

3   Language contained in deed to property owned by the "Chicago Lumbering Company."
4   1880 United States Census Records, Schoolcraft County, Michigan, Hiawatha Township, Household No. 185.
5   "Utopia in Upper Michigan," David C. Byers with the assistance of Willis Dunbar, The Quarterly Review of the Michigan Alumnus, Winter 1957, p.169.
6   "Lumberjacks and River Pearls, Jack Orr, Pioneer Tribune Publishing, December 1979, pp. 27-28.

**The Arcade Saloon, corner of Water and Pearl Streets,
Schoolcraft County Historical Society photo.**

Heffron's nefarious business ventures were actively opposed by the lumber company. Company president, Abijah Weston, feared loss of production and other negative economic repercussions created by drunken lumberjacks and mill hands. But the company's campaign to permanently shut down Heffron's saloon and bawdy house was orchestrated locally by company treasurer, John D. Mersereau, who despised Dan's business enterprises on moral grounds.

The company hired informants to spy on Heffron's business establishments and were ever ready to prosecute him for even minor infractions of the liquor law.[7] Heffron was no fool and he avoided obvious violations while continuing his illicit trade in gambling and prostitution.

During March of 1883, Dan Heffron was brought before Justice Amos Hill on charges of selling liquors without filing the required bonds during the final four months of 1882. Heffron demanded a jury trial and several witnesses were called to testify. A number of witnesses stated that they had patronized Heffron's establishment and had purchased whiskey. One person testified that he had bought a whole bottle of whiskey while others stated they were served glasses of the beverage at ten cents per glass. Conversely, a few witnessed testified that they were only served "temperance" drinks and tonics. When the case went to the jury the initial vote stood at two for a guilty verdict and four for acquittal. The four who voted for acquittal argued that the patrons might have only been served

7   Ibid, p.28.

"medicine."[8] Eventually the two jurors who were certain of guilt relented and Dan was a free man.[9]

Manistique's first county courthouse built in 1883 and destroyed by fire in 1901. Schoolcraft County Historical Society photo.

Although Dan had momentarily escaped justice in Manistique, he ran into trouble in Oshkosh, Wisconsin when traveling there with a prize fighter by the name of Pat McHugh from Steven's Point, Wisconsin. The "slugger," whose judgment was often impaired, was arrested for smashing up a drinking establishment. Dan was with McHugh at the time and the officers thought he looked suspicious. They searched Heffron and found a loaded revolver. Heffron was promptly arrested for carrying a concealed

---

8 "The Verdict," *Schoolcraft County Pioneer,* Manistique, Michigan, March 24, 1883, p.3.
9 *Schoolcraft County Pioneer*, March 24, 1883, p.3.

weapon and was later ordered to pay a fine of five dollars plus costs.[10] The editor of the *Pioneer* humorously commented about the incident in the paper: "There is a rumor here that one of the Schoolcraft County saloonists has been closely inspecting the cells of the Oshkosh jail."[11]

The Polls were open in Manistique on April 2, 1883 and the sale of alcohol was prohibited by law. It seemed that Heffron had finally miscalculated as customers were seen entering and leaving the Arcade Saloon during the entire day. Charges were immediately filed against both Daniel and Dennis Heffron for keeping an open saloon on Election Day. After being taken into custody, they appeared before Wright E. Clarke, Justice of the Peace. Bond was set at $400 each and the brothers were released pending a jury trial to be held on May 2, 1883. When the trial took place, the jury brought back a unanimous guilty verdict and Justice Clarke sentenced the men to a $25 fine and 90 days in jail. Heffron's lawyer appealed to circuit court. A second jury trial was conducted—this time before Circuit Court Judge Joseph Steere. Despite the overwhelming evidence of guilt, one juror steadfastly refused to convict. The result was a hung jury and the case was never retried.[12]

Mersereau also collected evidence relating to Dan's "house of ill fame" which was located just across the river in Hiawatha Township. An opportunity presented itself when Dan brought in contractors to complete work on the interior of the brothel. A.M. Mathews was hired to paint the interior of the bawdy house and Corwin Adkins performed carpentry work. In March of 1883 both men submitted sworn affidavits pertaining to what they witnessed while working at the "Heffron building." The upper floor of the brothel consisted of a bar where alcoholic beverages were served. A dance floor was located adjacent to the bar and five women who lived at the house were observed dancing with customers. Mathews stated that he overheard patrons negotiating with the women regarding the cost of illicit sexual services. The evidence was handed over to Schoolcraft County Prosecuting Attorney William Riggs who lodged criminal charges against Daniel, Dennis and Larry Heffron for "Keeping a House of Ill Fame."[13]

10 "Police News" *Oshkosh Daily Northwestern,* Oshkosh, Wisconsin, February 27, 1883, p4c3; See Also; *Schoolcraft County Pioneer,* March 10, 1883, p.2.
11 *Schoolcraft County Pioneer,* March 10, 1883, p.2.
12 Schoolcraft County Circuit Court Archives, Case No. 116, People v Daniel and Dennis Heffron, Keeping an Open Saloon on Election Day, April 3, 1883. See Also: "Justice Dealt Out" *Schoolcraft County Pioneer,* January 30, 1884, p.4.
13 Schoolcraft County Circuit Court Archives, Case No. 112, People v. Dennis, Larry and Dan Heffron, Keeping a House of Ill Fame, Filed March 13, 1883.

After an initial finding of guilty before Amos H. Hill, Justice of the Peace, the case was appealed to circuit court. But a strange thing happened on the date set for trial in circuit court. The sheriff was unable to locate seven of the material witnesses who had been subpoenaed to testify.[14] The trial was finally held during the January 1884 term of the Circuit Court and the jury returned a verdict of acquittal.[15]

Undaunted, Mersereau left no stone unturned in his efforts to close down the Arcade Saloon. In June of 1883 the Heffron brothers failed to purchase the required bonds from the county treasurer to legally sell alcoholic beverages. This time, charges were brought against Dennis Heffron "who pretends to be the proprietor of the Arcade saloon." A guilty verdict was first rendered before Justice Hill and upheld again in circuit court where Judge Joseph Steere presided. Heffron's lawyer appealed the case to the Michigan Supreme Court. On April 30, 1884 the court overturned the conviction due to the insufficiency of the original complaint. Prosecutor Riggs had failed to allege a specific act of selling alcoholic liquors to an identified individual.[16] The Heffron's winning streak in court continued.

Weary of endless legal battles, the owner of Manistique's lone watering hole must have concluded that there was safety in numbers. Dan created additional lots on the "flat iron block" and sold them to eager entrepreneurs. Before long, six additional saloons lined Pearl Street. The lumber company's singular efforts to turn Manistique into a dry community had come to naught, and by the early 1890s, twenty-nine drinking establishments were found within the city limits.[17]

Despite his brushes with the law, Dan tried to keep up his masquerade as a respectable businessman. In addition to selling lots on the flat iron block, Heffron purchased additional property on the west side of the Manistique River in close proximity to the new railroad. He subdivided the property and in May of 1887 began selling lots in what became known as the "Daniel Heffron Addition" to the City of Manistique.[18] Dan still maintained business connections in Cheboygan, Michigan where he owned a hotel which he leased.[19] And finally, inspired by his experiences with the justice

14   Ibid.
15   "Justice Dealt Out" *Schoolcraft County Pioneer,* January 30, 1884, p.4.
16   "The Northwestern Reporter," Volume 19, May 8-July 5, 1884, Robertson Howard, Editor. Saint Paul: West Publishing Company 1884, pp.170-171.
17   "Lumberjacks and River Pearls, Jack Orr, pp. 27-28.
18   *Semi-Weekly Pioneer,* Manistique, Michigan, May 20, 1887, p.1.
19   "Personal" *The Sunday Morning Star,* Manistique, Michigan, October 26, 1890, p.1.

system, Dan entered the bail bond business.[20] He pocketed ten percent of the required bail bond for each of his defendants who appeared for trial.

Local elections in 1888 brought major changes to Manistique. The Democratic Party candidates won several important county offices including Dennis Heffron, who was swept into power as Schoolcraft County Sheriff. With his brother advantageously installed as sheriff, Dan was able to carry on business at his notorious house with impunity. William Riggs was elected as prosecuting attorney but was loath to bring any charges against Heffron, having been foiled in court on three occasions. Frustration boiled over in the local press. Thomas J. MacMurray, publisher of the *Manistique News*, accused the prosecutor of corruption. The accusation led to a libel suit in which the publisher was acquitted. Even Wright E. Clarke, editor of the *Pioneer*, was convinced that juries in Schoolcraft County would not convict for liquor law violations.

> **BAWDY HOUSE IN TROUBLE!**
>
> **IMPORTANT ARRESTS.**
>
> Last Sunday night a complaint was made out and placed in the hands of Under-Sheriff McNamara and Deputy Moody against Daniel Heffron for keeping a house of ill-fame, with orders to pull the place and arrest all the inmates. The officers named called to their assistance two or three of the village police and went out to the house. There were several of our "city bloods" already, there others "smelled the mice" and turned back. The officers succeeded in arresting Daniel Heffron, May Brown, Esther Bassel, Frankie Smith, Winnie Gaylene, Carrie Beams and Kittie Adams. Carrie Beams being on the sick list was not brought to the cooler; but the others were landed there in due
>
> *Tri-Weekly Pioneer*, Nov. 9, 1891, p.1

Though Manistique was destined to have its share of saloons, the bawdy house was another matter. MacMurray kept up the pressure in the *Manistique News* and by 1891 public opinion was starting to sway. The citizens of Manistique had been shaken by events in nearby Seney and Trout Lake, where the violent shooting deaths of two Seney saloon owners, Stephen Harcourt and Dan Dunn, had made headlines across the state. Three years earlier in 1888, Dunn had stood trial in Manistique for running a house of ill repute at Seney, but was acquitted. Spurred on by the killings of Harcourt and Dunn, the authorities in Manistique resolved to act against Dan Heffron.

The trap was sprung on Sunday evening, November 8, 1891. With Sheriff Heffron out of town, a complaint was placed in the hands of Under Sheriff McNamara and Deputy Moody alleging that Dan Heffron was "keeping a house of ill fame." Orders were given to shut down the house and arrest the perpetrators. Three village police officers were enlisted to assist in the

---

20 "Dan Heffron Skipped" *Tri-Weekly Pioneer*, Manistique, Michigan, March 5, 1892, p.1.

raid. The surprise was complete, catching several of the female employees and their customers in the middle of their illicit transactions. The officers recognized many of the patrons and their names were added to the witness list. Apprehended in the raid were Daniel Heffron, Kitty Adams, Esther Basset, Carrie Beams, May Brown, Winnie Gaygue and Frankie Smith. Heffron was released on $3000 bail, but the women were all sent off to jail. An exception was made for Carrie Beams who was ill and was released on her own recognizance.[21]

Michigan Attorney General Adolphus Ellis, Courtesy Google Books

Dan was arraigned in Manistique on January 12, 1892 before Hon. Joseph H. Steere, Circuit Judge. After the charges were read by William Riggs, Prosecuting Attorney, Heffron stood mute and a "Not Guilty" plea was entered on his behalf. Heffron remained free on bail and the trial was set to begin at the end of February.[22]

Meanwhile, suspicions festered concerning Prosecuting Attorney Riggs and Sheriff Dennis Heffron. John D. Mersereau along with county supervisor Albert Hubbell, brought charges to Michigan Governor Edwin B. Winans against William Riggs, for "refusing and neglecting to entertain complaints against certain keepers of houses of ill fame" and they asked the governor to intervene. Winans dispatched Attorney General Adolphus A. Ellis to Manistique to conduct the investigation.[23] As the court opened a special session on February 29, Prosecuting Attorney Riggs continued to represent the People's case against Dan Heffron. However, Riggs stepped aside; pending the charges against him, and Attorney General Ellis took over for the People. The Attorney General

21 "Bawdy House In Trouble!" *Tri-Weekly Pioneer*, November 10, 1891, p.1.
22 Schoolcraft County Circuit Court Archives, Case No. 320, The People v. Daniel Heffron, Keeping a House of Ill Fame, Circuit Court Journal 1, pp. 226 and 339.
23 "Report of the Attorney General of the State of Michigan for the Year Ending June 30, A.D. 1893" Adolphus A. Ellis, Attorney General, Lansing, Robert Smith & Co., State Printers and Binders, 1893, p. 38.

presented a petition to the court alleging that Schoolcraft County Sheriff Dennis Heffron was incapacitated to act as Sheriff due to his relationship as a brother of the defendant. Judge Steere agreed and appointed Marshal Frank Jachor to act as Special Sheriff during the trial.[24]

The next order of business concerned a pressing issue with a member of the jury pool. Hiawatha resident, Francis G. Dodge reported to the court that he had been approached by George Tucker and was offered a $150 bribe to become a member of the jury panel and to render a corrupt verdict. Judge Steere issued a bench warrant against Tucker for Contempt of Court.[25]

The court then proceeded with the jury selection process. Once the jury was impaneled, the court ordered that they be sequestered for the remainder of the trial under the supervision of Special Sheriff Jachor.[26]

Testimony in the case went on for two days. Witnesses stated positive knowledge that Dan Heffron was the owner of the house, that he managed the business that was carried on there, and purchased the supplies that were used there. Some of the witnesses were patrons of the establishment and had the most intimate experience with the commerce that took place there. Wright E. Clarke, editor of the *Tri-Weekly Pioneer*, wrote that those who testified did not shy away from using plain language while on the witness stand. He lamented that the majority of the notes taken by his reporter who attended the trial were "so unfit for publication" that he was using them only as a reference.[27]

The defense witnesses were unable to make any inroads in the people's case. Dan Heffron testified in his own behalf, but withered under the masterful cross-examination of Attorney General Ellis. Many who attended the trial stated that absent any other evidence, Heffron's own testimony would have convicted him.[28]

The case went to the Jury on March 3 and most assumed a guilty verdict was a foregone conclusion. In about an hour word came that a verdict had been reached. Somehow, Dan received advance notice of the quick verdict and made good his escape. His whereabouts would remain forever unknown. It is possible that Dan ended up in San Francisco. A saloon

24 Schoolcraft County Circuit Court Archives, Case No. 320, Circuit Court Journal 1, p. 353.
25 Ibid, p.354.
26 Ibid, pp. 354-355.
27 "Dan Heffron Skipped" *Tri-Weekly Pioneer,* Manistique, Michigan, March 5, 1892, p.1.
28 Ibid.

keeper named Daniel Heffron resided there. He was the same age, and was born in Canada of Irish descent.[29] By 1912, he had immigrated back to Canada, and resided in Bow River, Alberta.[30]

After the trial, formal charges were also brought against Sheriff Dennis Heffron for neglect of duty, in connection with the house of prostitution which his brother owned. Attorney General Ellis conducted the investigation and a hearing was held at Manistique before Hon. Jerome Bowen, Judge of Probate of Schoolcraft County. Judge Bowen sustained the charges against the sheriff and sent them on to Governor Winans. However, no action was ever taken by the governor, and Heffron's term of office was allowed to quietly expire.[31] Heffron continued to reside in Manistique for many years, making his living as a saloon keeper. By 1910 he had moved to Aberdeen City, Washington where he also owned a saloon. He died in Milwaukee, Wisconsin in 1926 at age 65.

When Dan absconded from Manistique in March of 1892, he left his bail bondsman "holding the bag" to the tune of $5000. Prosecuting Attorney Riggs immediately brought suit against the "lands, tenements, goods, chattels, moneys and effects of Daniel Heffron" to recover the bail that was intended to insure his appearance at court. With charges still pending against Prosecutor Riggs for neglect of duty, he resigned his office and Carey W. Dunton was appointed as prosecutor in his place. The court attached all of Dan's real estate holdings in Schoolcraft County. After several legal delays, the properties were auctioned off to the highest bidder on the front steps of the county courthouse on December 12, 1892.[32]

---

29 1910 United States Census, San Francisco, California, Assembly District No. 84, Household No. 299.

30 1916 Canadian Census.

31 "Report of the Attorney General of the State of Michigan for the Year Ending June 30, A.D. 1892" Adolphus A. Ellis, Attorney General, Lansing, Robert Smith & Co., State Printers and Binders, 1892, p. 98.

32 Schoolcraft County Circuit Court Archives, Case No. 329, People v. Daniel Heffron, Attachment.

Chapter Six:
Pond v. The People

Just before dawn on June 18, 1859, the usually tranquil community at Seul Choix Point on Lake Michigan's northern shore was transformed into a murder scene. A fisherman lay dead—killed by his neighbor. The culprit was swiftly apprehended and handed over to the authorities for trial. The jury found the defendant guilty, and the case was appealed to the Michigan Supreme Court. The court's landmark ruling established a precedent for the state and the nation.

The rocky shore at Seul Choix. Photo courtesy Lee Ekblad.

In the 1850s the village at Seul Choix teemed with activity. The primitive dwellings of a large community of fishermen lined the narrow rocky shore. The clear blue water off the point offered a rich harvest of whitefish and lake trout, which every summer attracted an influx of fishermen.

Augustus Pond and his family traveled the 75 miles from Mackinac

Island by rowboat to engage in commercial fishing at Seul Choix. Pond, aged 34, was a peaceable man of French and Native American descent. He resided at Seul Choix with his wife Mary and their three young children, including a 12-year-old daughter Mary, a five-year-old son and a new baby boy.[1]

Augustus Pond, courtesy Robert Bloomfield.

Pond's humble home measured 16 feet square. It was a one-room, rough-hewn shanty with a bark roof, a window and a door. The door opened outward and was attached to the hut with leather straps used as hinges. It was secured by an attached rope tied around a pin inside the hut.[2]

Pond had one out-building: a net house that stood only 36 feet from his front door. This building was slightly smaller but of similar construction. Six posts were set in the ground and enclosed with one-inch boards nailed to the timbers. The roof was fashioned using poles and bark slabs. The building was floored with boards. A door faced Pond's hut and was held in place with leather hinges and secured with a rope. A sleeping berth that would accommodate two people comfortably was constructed on the wall opposite the door.[3]

Pond had two hired men, Daniel Whitney and Dennis Cull to assist him in his fishing operations. These servants ate their meals with the family in the hut, but slept at night in the net house.[4]

There were dozens of fishermen from St. Ignace, Mackinac Island and Beaver Island, who spent their summers fishing commercially at Seul Choix. Among them were David Plant, Joseph Robilliard and Isaac Blanchard, Jr. David Plant was an Irishman and a natural leader. He also was a heavy drinker and a bully. Robillard was his constant companion. Isaac Blanchard Jr., age 22, was the youngest member of the group. Blanchard was a giant of a man who stood six feet, seven inches tall and weighed over

---

[1] *Michigan Reports. Report of Cases Heard and Decided in The Supreme Court of Michigan from January 4 to October 13, 1860.* Thomas M. Cooley, Reporter. Vol. IV. Being Volume VIII of the Series. Ann Arbor: Published by the Reporter. Detroit: F. Raymond & Co. and S. D. Elwood. 1860. Augustus Pond v. The People. Page 151.
[2] Ibid. p. 151-152
[3] Ibid, p. 152
[4] Ibid.

240 pounds.[5] His super-human feats of strength were already legendary throughout the Eastern Upper Peninsula. Blanchard's father was a pioneer resident of Mackinac County and an influential Justice of the Peace on Mackinac Island.

David Plant, the leader of the group, developed an intense dislike for the passive Pond. On Thursday, June 16, 1859, around noon, Pond's daughter Mary strolled along the shore and passed near the home of the Downey family. She overheard Plant and Blanchard talking with Mrs. Downey. Plant, in a loud voice, threatened to whip Augustus Pond. Mary rushed home to tell her parents.[6]

That evening Plant, Robilliard and Blanchard went hunting for Pond. A gang of young ruffians followed along to watch. They found Pond at the home of Joseph Martell. Plant called for Pond to come outside. As soon as he emerged from the home the men surrounded him. Plant tried to bait Pond into a fistfight. He accused him of abusing his neighbors. When Pond remained silent he punched him in the face, knocking off his hat. Then he kicked him in the chest. Pond's only reaction was to retrieve his hat and place it back on his head.[7] Blanchard carried a bottle of whiskey that he shared with the others. While his tormentors drank, Pond took the first opportunity to run away into the woods.

Later that same evening around 10 o'clock, the three men searched for Pond again. The mob followed along. They arrived at Pond's net house where his two hired men slept inside. The door was closed and secured with a rope. The men tore the door from its leather hinges and Plant entered the net house. Blanchard and Robilliard waited outside. Whitney and Cull were heavy sleepers and did not awaken until they heard the sound of Plant walking on the floor. Plant grabbed Whitney by the arm only to discover he had the wrong man. The Irishman left the net house and proceeded to Augustus Pond's hut. Plant opened the unsecured door and walked into the home uninvited. Pond's terrified wife Mary and their children were inside.[8]

"Where is Gust Pond?" Plant demanded.

Mary told him to go check her husband's boat. Plant said that they had

---

5   "Man's Home His Castle" *Escanaba Daily Press,* Escanaba, Michigan, December 13, 1967, p. 16.
6   *Michigan Reports,* p. 153.
7   Ibid, p. 154.
8   Ibid.

already been to the boat and Pond was not there.

The Irishman told Mary he had business with her husband, but refused to explain further. After the three men left, Pond returned home undetected. He stayed for only five minutes before leaving again to spend the night with his neighbor, Joseph Martell.[9]

The following day, Pond avoided going back to his hut. He stopped by the Martell home in the morning to pick up his pistol, which he said he would give to his hired man. Around noon of the same day Pond came across Plant and Blanchard near the home of Peter Closs. Plant started harassing Pond again, and witnesses overheard him making threats to harm Pond. Pond remained silent in response to these threats and slipped quietly away. Plant walked over to the dock and told those present that he must whip Augustus Pond, or be called the world's biggest loafer.[10]

On Friday evening a nearly full moon illuminated the lakeshore. Pond's hired men, Whitney and Cull, repaired the door to the net house and went to bed around 10:00 p.m. Plant, Robilliard and Blanchard spent most of the evening drinking aboard their boat. They finally came ashore around 11:00 p.m. No one fell asleep in the home of Augustus Pond, for they feared that Plant and his friends would return.[11]

About 1:00 a.m. on Saturday morning, Plant, Robilliard and Blanchard went to the net-house where Whitney and Cull slept. Whitney was awakened by the creaking of boards being pried off the roof directly over his head. Cull continued sleeping. The three men had dismantled the west wall of the net-house and a portion of the roof. After Whitney woke up, the men stopped what they were doing and headed for Pond's front door. Plant grabbed the door and started shaking it. He demanded that someone open the door. He wanted to see the master of the house. Pond's wife Mary said that her husband was not inside, but Pond was inside hidden under the bed. Plant started shaking the door again.

"Open the door! We want to search the house."

"I told you he is not here," Mary replied.

Plant used several ploys to gain entrance into the hut, but Pond's wife steadfastly refused to admit him. The three men finally went away.[12]

---

9   Ibid. p. 155
10 Ibid. p. 156
11 Ibid.
12 Ibid. p. 157.

Pond took the opportunity to hurry over to the nearby home of his brother-in-law. There he obtained a double-barreled shotgun loaded with pigeon shot. He returned about fifteen minutes later with the gun. After briefly inspecting the damage to the net house, Pond went back inside his hut. Whitney did not go back to bed, but instead walked toward the home of Thomas Ward. Pond's other hired man remained asleep in the net house.[13]

Plant, Robilliard and Blanchard were already at the home of Thomas Ward. They were making a ruckus. Plant woke up the entire household even after being told there was a sick child inside. He demanded to come inside the house. Ward came outside instead to talk to Plant and keep the peace. The three troublemakers were drinking. Plant told Ward about tearing down Pond's net house, and he asked Ward to join them. They were going back to finish the job. They wanted to locate Pond, "whip him or even have his soul out of him." Ward refused to be part of it.[14]

Within a short time the drunken fishermen arrived back at the Pond family hut. They asked to come in but Pond's wife refused. The door was secured with the rope. Unable to get into the hut, the men turned their attention to the net house. Robilliard and Blanchard began ripping off more boards. Plant stepped inside where Cull was still sleeping soundly. Plant grabbed him and pulled him out of bed. Cull managed to cry out as he struggled to free himself. Pond heard the commotion and came out of his hut. He was armed with a shotgun.[15]

"Who is tearing down my net-house?" The only response was the screeching of boards as they were ripped away from the building.

"Leave or I'll shoot," shouted Pond, as more boards were torn loose. Thirty seconds passed.

"Leave or I'll shoot," Pond yelled again. There was no answer except the voice of Dennis Cull as he cried out in pain from inside the net house where Plant was assaulting him. The explosion of the shotgun blast rang out just before daybreak on Saturday, June 18, 1859.[16]

The body of Isaac Blanchard Jr. was found shortly after sunrise in the woods about 210 yards from Pond's hut. The strongman ran there before

---

13 Ibid. p. 158
14 Ibid. pp. 158-159.
15 Ibid. p. 159.
16 Ibid. pp. 160-161.

death overtook him. The mortal wound was inflicted by the burst of pigeon shot from Pond's gun. Only one barrel had been discharged.[17]

Grave of Isaac Blanchard.

Pond first went to see his brother Louis who was a constable. His brother refused to get involved. Pond wanted to turn himself into the authorities on Beaver Island about 25 miles away. Blanchard's father would have less influence there. Whitney and Cull accompanied Pond and helped row the boat. When they were within seven miles of Beaver Island they were stopped by another craft from Seul Choix. Pond was taken aboard that vessel and returned to the fishing village. From there he was brought to Mackinac Island as a prisoner.[18]

The trial was held two months later. Pond's attorney argued that the homicide was justifiable to defend his home against a felonious assault. The District Judge rejected the defense theory in his instructions to the jury. Pond was convicted of manslaughter and sentenced to ten years of hard labor at Jackson prison.[19]

Pond's attorney immediately appealed the case to the Michigan Supreme Court. The court found that the jury had been given incorrect instructions regarding justifiable homicide and self-defense. The landmark ruling came on May 19, 1860. It read in part:

"The guilt of the accused must depend on the circumstances as they appear to him, and he will not be held responsible for a knowledge of the facts, unless his ignorance arises from fault or negligence."[20]

"A man assaulted in his dwelling is not obliged to retreat, but may use such means as are absolutely necessary to repel the assailant from his house, or prevent his forcible entry, even to the taking of life. And if the

17 Ibid. p. 161.
18 Ibid. pp. 161-162.
19 Ibid. p. 168.
20 Ibid. p, 150.

assault or breaking is felonious, the homicide becomes at common law justifiable and not merely excusable." [21]

Pond had acted to prevent the destruction of his home and to save the life of his servant. A new trial was ordered and Pond was set free. The case was never retried. Pond died four years later. The cause of his death was not recorded.

In 1925, Dr. Ossian Sweet, an African American physician, purchased a home for his family at the corner of Garland and Charlevoix Avenues in Detroit. This was a working class all white neighborhood. The Sweet family moved into the home on September 8 of that year along with nine adult male friends and relatives. The men expected trouble and were armed. That same evening a crowd of white citizens gathered outside the residence to deliver the unmistakable message that the Sweets were not welcome. Sweet had grown up in Georgia and knew the danger posed by angry mobs. As a youth he had witnessed the ghastly specter of black men lynched. Dr. Sweet testified at his trial that when he saw the crowd, ". . . I realized that I was facing the same mob that has hounded my people throughout its entire history."[22]

The following night the mob returned. A reporter for the *Detroit News,* who was present covering the story, estimated the crowd between 400 and 500 people. Rocks were thrown at the house and two windows shattered. Almost immediately a shot rang out from inside the house, then seven or eight more in rapid succession. Leon Breiner, a neighbor, lay dead on his front porch—killed by a bullet fired from the Sweet home. The police, who were at the residence to protect the Sweets, entered the home and arrested the eleven adults. All were tried for murder or conspiracy to commit murder.

Famed trial attorney, Clarence Darrow, led the defense team. The legal basis for the defense was the principles set out by the Michigan Supreme Court in *Pond* v. *The People.* The trial of Dr. Sweet and the other defendants ended on November 27, 1925. The all male white jury deadlocked.

The prosecution wanted another trial. The defense successfully moved to have each defendant tried separately. Dr. Sweet's younger brother, Henry Sweet, was tried next. The second trial before another all white male jury

---

[21] Ibid.
[22] *Let Freedom Ring,* Arthur Garfield Hayes, New York: Livenright Publishing Corp. 1937 page 226.

began in May of 1926. Darrow eloquently confronted the issue of racial prejudice. He argued that the Sweets had a right to defend themselves in their own home: "They went there to live. They knew the dangers. Why do you suppose they took these guns and this ammunition and these men there? Because they wanted to kill somebody? It is utterly absurd and crazy [to think that]. They took them there because they thought it might be necessary to defend their home with their lives and they were determined to do it. They took guns there that in case of need they might fight, fight even to death for their home, for each other, for their people, for their race, for their rights under the Constitution and the laws under which all of us live; and unless men and women will do that, we will soon be a race of slaves, whether we're black or white." [23]

The twelve white jurors voted for acquittal. Henry Sweet was set free. The prosecution never retried the other defendants.

Though dead now for nearly 150 years, Augustus Pond's name lives on in the legal decision that continues to be upheld in Michigan and across the nation.

---

23 Closing argument of Clarence Darrow in People v. Henry Sweet in the Recorders Court, Detroit, Michigan, May 11, 1926. Transcript published by the National Association for the Advancement of Colored People.

Chapter Seven:
Utopia in the Northwoods

Abe Byers was a familiar figure on the streets of Manistique. He roamed the city boardwalks dressed in his "Sunday best" suit and tie, topped off with a derby hat. A cane flung over his shoulder passed through the handle of a valise filled with populist pamphlets. The Hiawatha township farmer was convinced that the current economic system was "all wrong." He told everyone he met of the merits of the Populist movement. Byers believed that capitalism was a rich man's system—designed for the benefit of the wealthy elite and the detriment of the wage earner.[1] These were radical ideas to espouse in the booming timber region. The Chicago Lumbering Company owned almost all the property and most of the businesses in town. The bemused company bosses must have looked upon "Uncle Abe" as a harmless eccentric—then the economy turned sour.

Abraham Byers, Schoolcraft County Historical Society, Sally Setterlind Collection

Abraham Sneathen Byers was born in Darke County, Ohio in March of 1829. By the early 1850's Abe had left home and moved to Indiana where, in 1852, he married Henrietta Lee. This union produced five children:

---

1   John I. Bellaire Manuscript, "Hiawatha Colony: Its Rise and Fall" p. 1, Bellaire Papers, Schoolcraft County Historical Society archives.

Elonzo, Viola, Fremont, Josephine and Abraham (Lincoln).[2] Tragically, Henrietta died in 1861 at age 31—only six weeks after giving birth to Lincoln. Abe's nephew, 15-year-old Harvey Booze, joined the family following the death of Abe's sister Catherine in 1856.[3] Sometime prior to 1866, the Byers family moved to Van Buren County, Michigan, where Abe purchased a farm near the town of Bangor.

Abe Byers married for a second time in 1866. His new wife, Elizabeth Kepler Reynard (Lizzie), was born near Winchester, Indiana in 1842.[4] She married a neighbor boy, Solomon Reynard, in September of 1862.[5] He left immediately after the wedding to fight in the Civil War. Reynard joined the 57th Indiana Infantry regiment and died six months later after being accidentally wounded at the Battle of Murfreesboro, Tennessee.[6] Abe's second wife bore him four more children.

Byers was a deeply religious man who lived by an unyielding moral code. He never smoked, drank, or used profanity. When Abe found his sons playing cards, which he associated with gambling, he imposed his own style of discipline. Abe abruptly ended the game by throwing the cards into the fire.[7] A strict observer of the Sabbath, Byers spent the Lord's Day in prayerful study of the Scriptures. Abe's ire was aroused one Sunday morning upon his return home from praying in the woods. To his horror, he discovered his wife Lizzie baking bread and his niece playing secular songs on the organ. Enraged, Byers threatened to chop the organ into firewood with his axe. An exasperated Lizzie brought the argument to a swift conclusion. She crowned Abe's righteous head with a bowlful of bread dough.[8]

After the crops were planted in the spring and whenever he could spare time away from the farm, Abe would travel throughout southwestern

[2] 1860 United States Census, Kosciusko County, Jackson Township, Indiana, Household Number 1436; See also: David C. Byers Manuscript, "Abraham Sneathen Byers and the Hiawatha Village Association," July 1, 1955, Schoolcraft County Historical Society archives.
[3] Olive M. Anderson, "Utopia in Upper Michigan," Northern Michigan University Press, Marquette, Michigan, 1982, p.1.
[4] *Manistique Pioneer Tribune,* Manistique, Michigan, "Fall Fatal to Pioneer of Hiawatha," November 9, 1933, p.1.
[5] National Archives, Civil War Widow's Pension File for Elizabeth A. Reynard, beneficiary of Solomon A. Reynard, 57th Indiana Infantry, Co. E; Randolph County Indiana Marriage License and Marriage Certificate dated September 4, 1862.
[6] National Archives, Civil War Widow's Pension File, Adjutant General, War Department, Medical History, B. P. McCain, Adjutant General, August 26, 1916.
[7] David C. Byers, "Abraham Sneathen Byers and the Hiawatha Village Association," p. 14.
[8] Olive M. Anderson, "Utopia in Upper Michigan," p. 6.

Michigan and northern Indiana as an itinerate preacher. By 1882, Abe decided it was time to explore new horizons. During August of that year, Abe and his nephew Harvey traveled to the Upper Peninsula in search of quality land for a homestead. They rode the train as far as McMillan, in present-day Luce County. From there, they donned their backpacks and tramped through the woods to Manistique. While in Manistique, they heard about some magnificent hardwood forests with clear spring water located about 12 miles north of town. Once Abe inspected the area, he knew he had found his future home. He proceeded to the land office in Marquette to put in claims for nine 160-acre parcels: one for himself and eight others for his relatives. These included his sons Lincoln, Elonzo, and Fremont; his son-in-law Ira Lobdell; his brother James Byers and his brothers-in-law John Kepler, Alva Kepler, and Eli Huey. The area became known as the Byers settlement.[9]

Two months later, in October of 1882, Abe chartered a railroad car into which he loaded all of the family's household goods, two horses, a cow, several crates full of chickens, and the pet dog, Jack. Only one person was allowed to ride in the boxcar to tend the stock. But on this occasion Abe deviated from his ethical values. Byers' 13 year old son Will was secreted into the car to ride with his father. Will hid under the hay at each stop, coming out only when the cars started to move again. Byers' wife Lizzie, his sons Lincoln and David, and Harvey's daughter, Alida rode the passenger cars north. At the Straits of Mackinac, the family boarded the steamer *Van Raalt* while their belongings and livestock were transferred from the boxcar. During their stormy cruise to Manistique, everyone became seasick except Lizzie.[10] The entire journey from southwestern Michigan to Manistique had taken seven days.[11]

The Byers' first home in the new settlement was a 24 feet by 30 feet log cabin. The family's first Upper Peninsula winter was a long one. A relative from Bangor shipped them a barrel of cornmeal which Lizzie made into mush. Abe's sons were skilled hunters and trappers. Game was plentiful and provided both food and income. Venison quarters and beaver pelts were sold to customers in Manistique.[12]

9 David C. Byers, "Abraham Sneathen Byers and the Hiawatha Village Association," p.1.
10 Ibid. p.4.
11 David C. Byers with the assistance of Willis F. Dunbar, "Utopia in Upper Michigan" The Story of the Hiawatha Village Association, The Quarterly Review of the Michigan Alumnus, Winter 1957, p. 169.
12 David C. Byers, "Abraham Sneathen Byers and the Hiawatha Village Association," p. 3.

When spring finally arrived, Byers and his sons began the laborious task of clearing the land. Crops were planted on the arable soil. Relatives from Van Buren County came north to join the settlement. David Byers remembered as many as 30 people at a time staying on their property until their own cabins were built and ready for occupation. The scene was repeated throughout the years, as Abe and Lizzie welcomed newcomers to the area.[13]

The experience of the Byers family was similar to that of other pioneers. Everyone had hardships to endure. One frigid winter day, Abe's oldest son Elonzo became lost in the woods while hunting. By the time he found his way back home, one foot and three fingers had to be amputated due to frostbite.[14]

Walter Thomas Mills, courtesy Wikimedia Commons

The Byers settlement grew and prospered during the 1880s. By the beginning of the 1890s, however, events in other parts of the country began to impact the local economy. It was at this time that Abe was drawn to the populist movement, an outgrowth of the cooperative Farmer's Alliance of the 1880s. The Populists were concerned about social and economic issues which adversely affected farmers. These were the identical issues that agitated Abe Byers. The People's Party was organized in Omaha, Nebraska on July 4, 1892 as an alternative to the Democrats and Republicans. The populist platform advocated numerous reforms, including government ownership of transportation; a national currency based on the unlimited coinage of both silver and gold; a graduated income tax; and an eight-hour work day.

Abe Byers became a tireless advocate for the People's Party cause. He stood on street corners in Manistique, extolling the virtues of the

13 Ibid. p.7.
14 Byers and Dunbar, "The Quarterly Review of the Michigan Alumnus, Winter 1957," p. 169.

party agenda while he peddled subscriptions to populist magazines and newspapers. Despite his best efforts, the editor of Manistique's *Weekly Tribune* speculated that the people were not ready "to turn their affairs over to the tender mercies of the Populists."[15]

But attitudes began to change following the Panic of 1893, which brought hard times to Schoolcraft County. The crisis started in February of that year with the bankruptcy of the Philadelphia and Reading Railroad and the subsequent failure of several banks. As the nation spiraled into a severe economic depression, industrial centers, mill towns, and farmers were the hardest hit. High rates for railroad transportation, currency inflation, and falling prices for agricultural products pinched the pocketbooks of local farmers.

As the depression stretched into 1894, Byers searched for solutions in populist publications. He happened upon a book by famed orator and temperance lecturer, Walter Thomas Mills, titled "The Product Sharing Village." Mills promoted the establishment of cooperative communities in which the residents would share equally in the fruits of their labor. Byers was so impressed by what he read that he wrote to Mills (who resided in Oak Park, Illinois) and offered to donate his land, along with that of his neighbors, for the creation of a cooperative colony in the U.P.[16] Amazingly, Mills accepted Abe's proposal, promising to come to Manistique and help with its implementation.

In March 1894, Abe went public with the plan, holding meetings in Manistique and in Hiawatha Township to recruit new families to join the commune.

Spurring residents to consider this cooperative arrangement was the state of the economy in the area; the downturn had severely impacted Manistique's largest employers, the Chicago Lumbering Company and the Weston Lumber Company. Lumberjack wages in the Upper Peninsula had been slashed from an average of $25 per month in 1893 to only $10 per month the following year.[17] The dramatic drop in income created discontent among local lumberjacks and mill workers. A meeting attended by up to 500 lumber company workers included speeches demanding restoration of the previous year's wages and a reduction in work hours. August Highland

---

15 *The Weekly Tribune,* Manistique, Michigan, April 15, 1894.
16 David C. Byers, "Abraham Sneathen Byers and the Hiawatha Village Association," p. 14.
17 Paul Kleppner, "The Cross of Culture: A Social Analysis of Midwestern Politics 1850-1900," New York, The Free Press, Div. of MacMillan Co., 1970, p.233.

and Abe's son, Beecher Byers, figured prominently in the meeting. They were authorized to submit a list of demands to the company bosses with a threat of a strike, if the resolutions were not acted upon.[18] The threatened stoppage did not materialize however, as most employees reported for work rather than risk losing their jobs.[19] Wages and work hours remained unchanged.

Rumors soon spread that Abe Byers had plotted behind the scenes to incite the labor unrest. The *Weekly Tribune* reported on April 12 that "Mr. A.S. Byers denies emphatically that he was the instigator of the strike." True or not, the damage was done. Byers' future cooperative community had acquired a powerful enemy.

Walter Thomas Mills arrived in the Upper Peninsula port city a few weeks later. He was an unusually small but distinguished-looking man with mutton-chop sideburns. Though short in stature, he was a powerful and eloquent speaker.[20] He delivered a series of lectures at the Star Opera House that were enthusiastically received and swayed local opinion in favor of the enterprise.

In short order, several members of the Byers clan deeded their farms to the colony, legally known as the "Hiawatha Village Association." These included Abe Byers; his sons Elonzo, Lincoln, Beecher, and William; and Byers' brothers-in-law, the Keplers, and Eli Huey.[21] Individuals who donated their land agreed to move into association housing as soon as it was ready.[22]

Several newcomers also embraced the cooperative, including many of Mills' friends and relatives from Iowa. Another social activist from Chicago, John Henry Randall, and his family joined them a year later in the spring of 1895. Randall had recently led an army of marchers to Washington, D.C. to protest the widespread unemployment.[23]

Throughout the summer and fall of 1894, Hiawatha Village was transformed from an idealized concept to a physical reality. At its peak, the

18 "Threatened Strike," *Semi-Weekly Pioneer,* Manistique, Michigan, April 11, 1894, p.1.
19 *Semi-Weekly Pioneer,* April 14, 1894.
20 John I. Bellaire Manuscript, "Hiawatha Colony: Its Rise and Fall"
21 Olive M. Anderson, "Utopia in Upper Michigan," p. 18-19
22 Charlotte R. Byers, "The Hiawatha Colony: A Story of Its Rise and Fall," *Escanaba Daily Press,* Escanaba, Michigan, December 13, 1931, p. 11.
23 Charlotte R. Byers, "History of the Hiawatha Colony Written by One of Its Members," *Escanaba Daily Press,* December 10, 1931, p. 6. See Also, *The Industrial Christian,* Hiawatha, Michigan, March 2, 1895.

colony numbered approximately 225 men, women, and children.[24] Assets included 1,080 acres of land, 125 cattle, and 25 horses.[25]

The ringing of the woodman's axe and the rhythmic hum of the cross-cut saw were heard throughout the village. Land was cleared for crops, and cabins were constructed for arriving families. The homes were laid out in the shape of a horseshoe with a center courtyard and water well.[26] Use of alcoholic beverages was forbidden on the grounds, and several members voluntarily gave up their tobacco habits as well.

A community store was established for the purchase of needed items. One hour of labor was equal to one time credit, which could be used to purchase supplies at the store. Individuals who donated $1,000 in real estate or personal property were exempted from labor and automatically granted time credits. Individuals who were unable to work were also provided with a set number of time credits.[27] A stage traveled to Manistique three times per week and brought back supplies to be re-sold at the store using time credits. The association also purchased staples such as flour, sugar and coffee which were portioned out to the colonist based upon the size of each family.[28]

The men of the commune were given a choice among several work assignments including the sawmill, dairy or agricultural departments; shoe shop; or print shop where the association newspaper, *The Industrial Christian*, was produced. Mills procured a contract from an outside business to produce cant hook poles and peavey shafts for use in lumbering.[29] The colony also had its own blacksmith shop and woodworking establishments.

The women of the colony were also busily engaged in communal work projects. Two women started a laundry, while others labored in soap-making and sewing rooms. Knitted items were manufactured on a machine. Deer hides were tanned and transformed into mittens, shoes, and jackets.[30]

The harvest in the fall of 1894 and 95 yielded bumper crops of potatoes and onions. Regrettably, this produce rotted in the cellars for lack of a local

---

[24] David C. Byers, "Abraham Sneathen Byers and the Hiawatha Village Association," p. 17.
[25] *Semi-Weekly Pioneer,* August 11, 1894.
[26] Ibid.; See Also: David C. Byers, "Abraham Sneathen Byers and the Hiawatha Village Association," p. 17.
[27] Byers and Dunbar, "The Quarterly Review of the Michigan Alumnus, Winter 1957, p. 172.
[28] Charlotte R. Byers, *Escanaba Daily Press,* December 13, 1931, p. 11.
[29] Byers and Dunbar, "The Quarterly Review of the Michigan Alumnus, Winter 1957, p. 172
[30] Ibid.

market and exorbitant rates for transportation. The Chicago Lumbering Company, which employed hundreds of hungry lumberjacks in the numerous camps scattered throughout Schoolcraft County, refused to purchase the colony products at any price. They also held a near monopoly on shipping by water and charged more for transportation than the produce would sell for in Milwaukee or Chicago.[31]

Abe's daughter-in-law, Charlotte Randall Byers, was 18 years old when she joined the colony in the spring of 1895. She recalled that during the summer the children spent their day gathering brush for a bonfire. During the evening the colonists would gather around the fire and the children would play old time games such as squat tag and drop the handkerchief. The adults sang popular songs of the day with the accompaniment of a musician playing a mouth organ or guitar, until one by one, the families wandered off to bed.[32]

**John and Evila Kepler, Annis Repp
Carney Collection**

Holidays were happy times in the colony. On July 4, 1895, the villagers were summoned from their beds at 4:00 a.m. by several rifle volleys fired on the center green. After the families had gathered around the well, Civil War veteran John Kepler recited the Declaration of Independence and the colonists sang "*My Country Tis of Thee.*" Then everyone went off to breakfast to prepare for a day of celebration. Charlotte remembered that the young couples had been assigned the task of making ice cream. They were provided with three empty fifty pound lard cans into which they mixed milk, cream, eggs, sugar and flavoring. The

---

31 Walter Thomas Mills, "Hiawatha Colony: A Story of Its Rise and Fall," *Escanaba Daily Press,* December 16, 1931, p. 5.
32 Charlotte R. Byers, *Escanaba Daily Press,* December 11, 1931, p. 5.

cans were placed in large tubs and surrounded with ice water and salt. By continuously moving the cans back and forth the ingredients were gradually transformed into a delicious slushy ice cream.[33]

By the spring of 1895, dissension began to set in. The colonists, including many newcomers from Iowa, had just emerged from a long cold Upper Peninsula winter. There also must have been lingering disappointment regarding the failure to find a ready market for the previous year's potato harvest. Both Charlotte Byers and Abe's son David point to controversy caused by "outsiders." Many of the villager's neighbors were suspicious of Walther Thomas Mills and they started rumors that the cooperative community was just a scheme by Mills to enrich himself and gain control of the colonist's property.[34] The first sign of discord occurred when two association members, John and Alva Kepler, declined to move into association housing. The Keplers were Civil War veterans who steadfastly refused to give up their homes despite Abe Byers' efforts to convince them otherwise. In the midst of the crisis, Mills consulted a lawyer in Chicago who advised him that the association could force the Keplers to move. When Mills and members of the commune showed up at the home of John Kepler, he greeted them at the door with a shotgun. Other members slipped in though the rear entrance and started moving out the furniture.[35] Kepler's wife, Evila, rushed forward to protest. In the melee that followed, Evila was shoved aside by Mills and "handled pretty roughly."[36] The Keplers' belongings were taken away and their cabin dismantled.

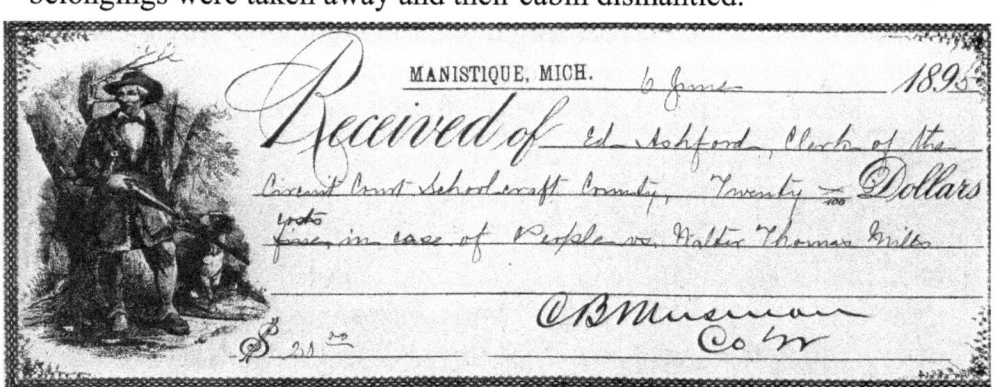

Schoolcraft County Circuit Court Archives

33 Charlotte R. Byers, *Escanaba Daily Press,* December 12, 1931.
34 Charlotte R. Byers, *Escanaba Daily Press,* December 13, 1931. p. 11.
35 Ibid.
36 "Making It Hot for Walter Thomas Mills," *Semi-Weekly Pioneer,* May 4, 1895, p. 1.

A tearful Kepler went to the home of fellow veteran Francis Dodge for advice. Dodge was a highly respected citizen of Hiawatha Township who had decided not to join the association. Mills had visited Dodge's home during the initial efforts to organize the Hiawatha Village Association in the spring of 1894. At some point during the conversation Mills told Dodge he would be "compelled" to join. Dodge, who was a rugged individualist, took exception to Mills' implied threat. The conversation ended abruptly when Dodge pointed to his rifle and told Mills that he would "make no cripples" should anyone invade his property. Dodge drove Kepler 10 miles "over sand ruts and corduroy roads" to the county seat in Manistique, where they met with the prosecuting attorney.[37] Arrest warrants were then issued for Walter Thomas Mills and four other association members. All were charged with assault and battery.

Mills' trial was held on May 3, 1895 in Manistique. He was required to pay a $50 fine and $20 in court costs or serve 90 days in jail.[38] Kepler also filed suit to have his farm property returned to him. In an attempt to mend the rift, the entire colony turned out to rebuild the family's log cabin.

However, with the Kepler precedent set, more members brought suit against the association, and each time association property was restored to the original owner and costs were assessed. Other members chose not to bring suit, but left to pursue more lucrative employment opportunities elsewhere. In the fall of 1895, with the prospect of enduring another Upper Peninsula winter, and a cash crop of onions rotting in the cellars for lack of a market, Mills and his friends and relatives from Iowa also abandoned the colony. When Mills resigned as President of the association, Abe's son David assumed the position and was left with the task of sorting out the association's affairs.

Each member who decided to pull out was provided with assets that would be nearly equal to the personal property, cash or stock that they had initially invested. Both David and Charlotte reported that there were few arguments and no "hard feelings." Mills, his parents, brothers and sisters lost everything that they had put into the colony, but the association sold some of the stock "to help them get away."[39]

---

37 Clint Dodge, "Hiawatha's 'Co-operative' Community Recalled By Former Local Resident" *Manistique Pioneer Tribune,* Manistique, Michigan, October 12, 1961.
38 "The People v. Walter Thomas Mills," Schoolcraft County Circuit Court Archives
39 Byers and Dunbar, "The Quarterly Review of the Michigan Alumnus, Winter 1957, p. 174.

In little more than a year's time, the experiment in Upper Peninsula communal living effectively drew to a close.

Mills blamed the failure of the colony on the opposition of the Chicago Lumbering Company, which he referred to as "a great business corporation owned by nonresidents and controlled by absent owners." The lumber company held a monopoly on almost every item the colony's residents needed to purchase to supply the colony store and when it came time to sell a cash crop of nine thousand bushels of potatoes "as fine as were ever grown," the lumber company was the only buyer—and they refused "at any price." The lumber company also controlled the shipping and set the freight rates higher than the market value of the products.[40]

Abe's son David Byers discounted the lumber company as the cause of the association's failure. Instead, he cited poor business practices along with an even more basic reason for the failure of the colony: the nature of man. As he explained, "They want constant struggle to get ahead of the other fellow" and they "won't do their best if they think the other fellow is going to share some of the harvest."

Abe Byers had contributed 160 acres, his team of horses, several head of cattle and a large flock of chickens to the association. He lost all the personal property he invested and his farm land was reduced by 40 acres. After a few years, the only original association settlers remaining in Hiawatha Township were Abe and Lizzie Byers and John and Evila Kepler. Abe and Lizzie lived out their lives on the old homestead staying with Abe's son Len and daughter-in-law Charlotte who had moved back to Hiawatha from Chicago to care for them. Abe died in 1913 while Lizzie lived on to the age of 90, passing away in November of 1933 from injuries sustained in a fall. Mills moved west and established another cooperative colony in Washington, but it too ended in failure.

Many of the policies advocated by the Populists including an eight-hour work day, a secret ballot and the direct election of U.S. Senators eventually became law. Though often thought of as eccentric, it is the dreamers who agitate for change who push society forward. Hiawatha Township had such a man in Abe Byers.

---

40 Walter Thomas Mills, *Escanaba Daily Press,* December 16, 1931, p.5.

Chapter Eight:
Portrait of an Altar Artist

Reared in a remote Upper Peninsula lumbering settlement, August Klagstad toiled in the mill piling pine slabs. But the high-pitched whine of the big saws could not drown out his dreams for a brighter future. When he exchanged his leather work gloves for brushes and a palette of oils—an artist emerged. A faithful Lutheran, Klagstad specialized in religious paintings. Today, Klagstad's altar paintings can be found in churches throughout the United States. His "sermons on canvas" have inspired generations of worshipers in Michigan and across the nation.

August Klagstad was born in Modum, Norway on August 14, 1866, the seventh of nine children of Torger and Karen Klagstad.[1] August's grandfather, Christian Klagstad was a talented carpenter who crafted high quality wagons and sleighs. August's father, on the other hand, tilled the worn-out Norwegian soil and struggled to provide for his growing family. By 1871, Klagstad's parents reached a momentous decision—they would immigrate to America.

The family, including five year old August and three of his siblings departed Drammen, Norway during the first week of May, 1871. The three oldest children remained behind until there was money enough to send for them. The emigrants set sail on the bark *Flora,* rather than a faster, more expensive steamship. Calm winds extended their crossing to seven weeks.[2]

On the 4th of July, 1871, the Klagstads finally arrived at their destination in Racine, Wisconsin. While in Racine, August's father heard that a lumber company in Monistique, (later known as Manistique) wanted laborers to work in the mill. Free transportation was provided on the schooner *Express.*[3]

1 August Klagstad, *Klagstad-Halverson Family History,* Minneapolis, Minnesota, August, 1946, p.3.
2 Ibid. p.4.
3 Ibid, p. 8.

Once the schooner arrived at the dock in Manistique, the family peered out on the forlorn landscape. A sawdust road led from the harbor to the settlement, which consisted of a saw mill, company store and a half-dozen unpainted houses. Karen Klagstad could not contain her dismay. After cheerfully enduring all the hardships of the long ocean voyage and the journey inland, she sat down by the side of the road and wept.[4]

The frontier hamlet of Monistique in 1871. *Klagstad-Halvorsen Family History*

But the Klagstads soon cast aside their disappointment and began building a life in the pioneer community. August's father labored 11 hours a day in the mill earning a dollar and a half per day.[5] Meanwhile, Karen Klagstad tended the children, cooked the meals, fashioned the family's clothing from fabric purchased at the store, and knit mittens and stockings from wool she spun herself.[6]

Manistique had no facilities for the education of children. School buildings and churches were non-existent. So August's mother taught her young ones to read and write in their native language. Their studies included Luther's Catechism and Bible history.[7]

A band of Ojibwa Indians lived a few miles from the settlement along the shore of an inland lake. The Indians had been converted to Christianity by Father Frederick Baraga in 1832. In 1873, the little Mission church built by the tribe and dedicated by Father Baraga, still stood on the shores of what later became known as Indian Lake. The Indians were frequent

4   Ibid.
5   Ibid, p. 4, 12.
6   Ibid. p. 13.
7   Ibid, p. 15.

visitors to the settlement and peddled assorted food items including wild blueberries, raspberries, maple sugar and venison. The women made baskets and moccasins which they brought to town for sale. Klagstad fondly recalled rambling over to the Indian village to trade for bows and arrows which be paid for with large apples from his mother's barrel.[8]

A dramatic change in the lives of the people of Manistique took place in 1872, when the lumber company was purchased by a group of New York businessmen led by Abijah Weston. Several new families moved into the community and improvements soon followed. The old mill was torn down and replaced with a larger, more modern facility. A new company store carried expanded stock. More company housing, a school building and a boarding house were erected.[9] The spiritual needs of the community also gained attention. Martin Quick, the new mill foreman and a devout Baptist, started a Sunday school.[10]

Religious services were first conducted in Manistique in the early 1870s by traveling clergymen known as "circuit-riders." Rev. Thomas J. MacMurray, a Methodist minister, rode a circuit from Wisconsin and preached in Manistique about once per month at the new school house. Klagstad vividly remembered one sermon on the "Evils of Intemperance." MacMurray portrayed a drunken father, arriving home to abuse his wife and children. Taking the oil lamp from the teacher's desk, MacMurray held it out at arm's length as his body trembled with emotion. Klagstad was convinced the lamp's glass chimney would fall to the floor and shatter. Multi-talented, MacMurray also published several volumes of poetry, obtained a law degree, and during the early 1890s left the ministry for a time to publish a newspaper in Manistique. His gift of a volume of his poetry became one of Klagstad's treasured possessions. MacMurray's famous grandson, screen actor Fred MacMurray, carried on the family's dramatic tradition.[11]

Klagstad's artistic talent came to the fore at an early age. He became friends with Elmer and Fred Colwell, whose father was the new superintendent of the lumber company. The attic of the Colwell home was filled with toys including a rocking horse, printing press and a primitive

---

8   Ibid, p. 40-41.
9   Ibid. p. 16, 20.
10 Ibid, p. 20; See also: *A Genealogy of the Quick Family In America* (1625-1942), By Arthur Craig Quick, Privately Published by Arthur C. Quick, South Haven and Palisades Park, Michigan, 1942 p. 225
11 August Klagstad, *Klagstad-Halverson Family History*, p. 30, 32.

"movie machine" called a zoetrope. The movie toy consisted of a round box with holes around the side, and strips of paper inside the box. By spinning the box on an axis and looking through the holes one could see a horse gallop, a dog jump or a man run. When the movie machine had seen its last days, Klagstad designed a new one using "round paper collar boxes" and drawing a sequence of images on strips of paper.[12]

Klagstad's idyllic boyhood years in Manistique were filled with outdoor fun. Summers were spent going barefoot, swimming, playing baseball, and games like "two old cat" and "pom pom pullaway." Klagstad enjoyed learning and attended class during the school term. The arrival of winter provided opportunities for sledding and ice skating.[13] But his early years were also touched with sorrow when his good friend, Freddy Colwell, died from a childhood disease.[14]

The grave of Fred Cowell, Lakeview Cemetery, Manistique.

In April of 1880, Wright Clarke, a journalist from Indiana, arrived in Manistique and started a newspaper, the *Schoolcraft County Pioneer*. Clarke wrote all the articles, set the type and printed each page, one at a time, on a hand press. Thirteen year old August Klagstad was hired to run the ink roller over the type while Clarke hand pressed each page. The *Pioneer* was the first newspaper ever published in Schoolcraft County, and young Klagstad was proud of his role in the benchmark event.[15]

12 Ibid. p. 38-39.
13 Ibid. p. 20.
14 Ibid. p. 39.
15 Ibid. p. 36.

As more Scandinavians moved to the burgeoning lumber town in search of jobs, there were sufficient numbers to justify inviting a Lutheran minister to Schoolcraft County to conduct worship services. The first Lutheran church service in Manistique was held in the parlor of the Klagstad home.[16] A Scandinavian Lutheran congregation was not formally organized and a church building erected until 1885. Klagstad was in the church's first adult confirmation class.

Northern Indiana Normal School, Courtesy Valparaiso University Library.

The course of Klagstad's life was unexpectedly altered while clearing land on his father's homestead. He was chopping down a tree when the ax slipped, cutting his foot. No longer able to work until his injury healed, he returned to school for the remainder of the winter. Klagstad was behind the other students, but his teacher, Nellie Coleman, quickly recognized his innate intelligence and placed him in the advanced class. Coleman was a dedicated educator who provided the one on one instruction necessary so he could catch up with his classmates. With his teacher's encouragement and the support of his mother, Klagstad decided to pursue an advanced education rather than spend his life laboring for the lumber company. When Klagstad did return to work in the mill, all of his earnings were saved for his future education.[17]

In the fall of 1886, Klagstad left Manistique to attend the Northern Indiana Normal School (now Valparaiso University) in Valparaiso,

16 Ibid. p. 35.
17 Ibid. p. 41.

Indiana.[18] He enrolled in the Preparatory Department with the intention of gaining future employment as a bookkeeper. But the normal school also had an excellent Fine Arts Department whose faculty included Professor Felix Ekblad, an accomplished artist from Sweden.[19] Ekblad observed Klagstad's natural artistic ability and encouraged him to develop his skills.[20] So inspired, Klagstad obtained employment at a studio in Chicago and took art lessons on Saturdays. He studied at both the Art Institute in Chicago and the Chicago Academy of Fine Arts. He later worked in art studios in New York and Boston and visited museums and art galleries throughout Europe.[21]

Gethsemane, Zion Lutheran Church, Manistique, Michigan

Klagstad's first altar painting was completed in Manistique in August of 1893 while vacationing from Chicago. The painting, "Christ in Gethsemane" was a copy of a work by celebrated German artist Heinrich Hofmann. Klagstad used a black and white photo of the original and relied on his own artistic creativity to select the colors.[22] The painting first adorned the altar of the Norwegian Danish Lutheran Church in Manistique, and has

18 *Semi-Weekly Pioneer,* Manistique, Michigan, November 3, 1885, p. 1; See also: *Semi-Weekly Pioneer,* November 5, 1886, p. 1.
19 Valparaiso University Archives, Indiana State Normal School 1885 Course Catalog, p. 20
20 Jane Kemp, "August Klagstad Biography," Luther College, Decorah, Iowa; July, 2004, p. 1.
21 N. N. Ronning, "August Klagstad, Artist" *The Friend* magazine, March, 1938, p. 20; See also, "Artist Who Painted Pictures Moves," *Escanaba Daily Press,* August 31, 1915, p. 3; See Also, Jane Kemp, "August Klagstad Biography" p.1
22 "A Work of Art" *Semi-Weekly Pioneer,* Manistique, Michigan, August 10, 1893, p.1

continued on display in houses of worship for over 120 years.

After moving to Marinette, Wisconsin, in 1895, Klagstad opened a studio there and did a booming business in finishing of photographic portrait enlargements. He also began to specialize in both portrait painting and religious art. His altar paintings were replicas of works by the masters which were well-known to church goers of his day. Klagstad added his own original colors and background details.

In August of 1897, Klagstad married Othelia Ness in a ceremony at the Lutheran Church in Manistique.[23] This union produced four children, Arnold, Rudolph, Alice and Leslie, all born in Marinette.[24]

Klagstad moved his studio from Marinette, Wisconsin to Minneapolis, Minnesota in 1915. There he expanded his studio operations to include church furnishings and pews. Two of his sons, Leslie and Arnold Ness Klagstad joined his studio in 1938. Arnold Klagstad became a talented and well-known artist in his own right, while Leslie managed the furnishing side of the business.

Klagstad advertised his altar paintings and furnishings in numerous church publications including the *Methodist Year Book*, the *American Baptist Year Book* and the *Lutheran Almanac*. He also printed a catalog to display his works.

Throughout the years, Klagstad maintained contact with relatives and associates in his native Norway. He traveled back to his homeland during the 1890s and again in the 1930s. He founded a society for Norwegians from his home province of Modum and also belonged to the Sons of Norway.[25] In 1946, spurred on by a desire to preserve the knowledge of his Norwegian heritage for future descendants, Klagstad completed the *Klagstad-Halvorsen Family History*. In it, he not only outlined his family genealogy, but also shared his memories of growing up in Manistique.

The influx of immigrants from Scandinavia to the United States in the 1880s and 1890s spurred a period of church construction. Klagstad's altar paintings fulfilled the need to adorn these newly constructed churches with religious art that was both appealing and affordable for the working-class Scandinavian congregations of his day.

---

23 "Marriage At Manistique," *The Sentinel,* Milwaukee, Wisconsin; August 30, 1897, p. 8.
24 1910 United States Census, Marinette County, Wisconsin, Marinette City, 4th Ward, p.. 6751
25 August Klagstad, *Klagstad-Halverson Family History*, p. 15.

***Saving Peter*, Norwegian Lutheran Church, Calumet, Michigan.**

During his long career, August Klagstad produced over 1000 altar paintings which were shipped to churches throughout the United States, as well as Canada, Norway, Australia and Africa. During an Interview in 1938, Klagstad revealed that his most popular church paintings were *Christ Knocking at the Door, In Gethsemane* and *Come Unto Me*.[26] Klagstad also painted portraits of local businessmen and dignitaries. For pleasure and relaxation, he switched from oils to watercolors to create noteworthy landscapes.

Many of Klagstad's paintings have fascinating histories of their own. Sometime prior to 1919, Klagstad accepted a commission to reproduce

26 N. N. Ronning, *The Friend,* March 1938, p. 20.

Eduard von Gebhardt's "*The Last Supper*" for the First Lutheran Church in Portland, Maine. The painting was displayed above the altar in the sanctuary. Disaster struck in December of 1925, ten days before Christmas. A four-story brick structure next to the church caught fire and was rapidly engulfed in flames. The inferno spread to the adjacent church building, igniting the shingles. Before the fire could be brought under control, the church roof had collapsed into the sanctuary. The next morning, members of the congregation sifted through the rubble. The organ in the rear of the auditorium was completely destroyed by falling debris, but to the delight of the parishioners, Klagstad's painting was discovered unharmed. When the roof caved in, heavy beams had fallen across the altar, completely shielding the artwork from the flames and fire hoses.[27] The painting continues on display today in the new church sanctuary.

August Klagstad died in March of 1949 in Minneapolis at the age of 82, but his art lives on in communities large and small. The images serve as visual testimonies of his strong religious faith. Klagstad loved poetry, and his favorite was *When Earth's Last Picture is Painted* by Rudyard Kipling—which he committed to memory.[28] The final lines capture the heart of an artist:

>And no one will work for the money.
>
>No one will work for the fame.
>
>But each for the joy of the working,
>
>And each in a separate star,
>
>Will draw the thing as he sees it,
>
>For the God of things as they are.

---

27 Elaine Killelea, *History of First Lutheran,* First Lutheran Church, Portland, Maine, August, 1999.

28 N. N. Ronning, *The Friend,* March 1938, p. 20.

Chapter Nine:
The Pioneer Life of Elizabeth Allen

Destined for a life of adventure, Elizabeth Allen's incredible journey began with her birth on a canal boat near Rochester, New York on February 15, 1853.[1] Her intrepid spirit sustained her during the challenging times that lie ahead. Whether sailing through a gale on Lake Michigan or riding into a dense wilderness to deliver the mail, Elizabeth's courage and determination never wavered.

Elizabeth's father, Reuben Allen was born in Franklin County, New York on June 1, 1831.[2] He moved to Rochester, New York in 1850 and worked with his father as a shoemaker.[3] There he met and married Margaret Gray. Soon after Elizabeth's birth in 1853, the family moved to Chicago where Reuben found work as a carpenter. When Margaret's health deteriorated after contracting typhoid fever, the family relocated further north to the Garden Peninsula in Upper Michigan. There they joined Mrs. Allen's parents, David and Isabelle Gray, who had already settled in the sparsely populated pioneer community.[4]

The Allen's first home was located at Garden Bay near two creeks. Reuben hewed out a log cabin on the lakeshore before finding work in the lumber industry at Sturgeon River and later at Big Bay de Noc.[5] But Elizabeth's father could not resist the lure of Lake Michigan with its rich abundance of lake trout and whitefish.

---

[1] "Mail Was Brought Here On Horseback in 1868 By Manistique Woman" *Escanaba Daily Press,* Escanaba, Michigan, April 12, 1931, p.13. See Also, "Pioneer Woman Is Called By Death" *Manistique Pioneer Tribune,* Manistique, Michigan, September 5, 1934, p.1
[2] The Garden Peninsula Historical Society, *Our Heritage,* 1982, p. 194.
[3] Ibid. See Also: 1850 United States Census, 4th Ward, City of Rochester, New York, Dwelling No. 168.
[4] The Garden Peninsula Historical Society, *Our Heritage,* 1982, p. 194. See Also, *Escanaba Daily Press,* April 12, 1931, p.13
[5] The Garden Peninsula Historical Society, *Our Heritage,* 1982, p. 194.

A two-masted Mackinaw boat in Manistique harbor. Photo Courtesy Schoolcraft County Historical Society, William Crowe Collection

Reuben built a boat of his own for use on the lake. The two-masted, flat bottom Mackinaws were favored among fishermen. Averaging 25 to 30 feet in length, these light weight sailing ships were capable of hauling heavy loads. The vessels handled well in all kinds of weather and the flat bottom enabled them to be put ashore almost anywhere.[6] Likewise, the fisherman's nets were hand crafted and much care was taken in their use and preservation. They were anchored in the water by hammering notches in stones and securing them to the bottom of the mesh with a slip knot and a short section of rope. Wooden floats were attached to the top of the nets to keep them upright in the water. After each catch the nets had to be brought ashore to dry and the wooden floats replaced, otherwise they would become waterlogged and sink to the bottom.[7]

While just a girl, Elizabeth sailed out on the lake with her father to help harvest the catch. Standing in the stern of the boat and wearing spike soled shoes to keep from slipping on the wet, greasy deck, she helped hoist up the nets, laden with trout and whitefish. Once they were ashore, Elizabeth worked alongside her dad cleaning and salting the fish and packing them into barrels.[8] The casks were purchased from local coopers and held 100 pounds of fish which were immersed in brine. The preserved fish were eventually sold to trading schooners from Chicago in exchange for cash or

6 Ibid., p. 15
7 Ibid.
8 *Escanaba Daily Press,* April 12, 1931, p. 13

staples such as flour and sugar.⁹

Elizabeth's family eventually moved to Sac Bay on the western shore of the Garden Peninsula. Here, her father built a ship for use as a trading vessel. Reuben purchased clothing and needed supplies in Green Bay and sold them in fishing ports all along the northern shore of Lake Michigan as far east as Mackinaw City.¹⁰ Elizabeth, being the oldest, always traveled with her father on these sailing expeditions. Elizabeth loved the lake and before long she became familiar with all the settlements along the shore and on the scattered islands. The vessel encountered many perilous storms but Elizabeth and her father were experienced mariners with the skills necessary to pilot their ship to safe harbor.¹¹

During the 1860s, mail service to the scattered ports and hamlets in the Garden Peninsula and points east along the lakeshore was intermittent at best. A Delta county resident named Harry Hutchins had a sailing ship called the *Blackhawk* which he used for carrying merchandise and also the mail.¹² The mail packets were brought from Escanaba to Garden by boat, and then delivered to the lumbering hamlet of "Monistique" either by horseback or on foot. Hutchins took a trail through the wilderness first tread by Indians and French fur traders. The route was known locally as the Portage Trail.¹³

The path through the woods was narrow and hard to follow. Civil War veteran James Lyon took the trail on one occasion when Hutchins was unable to make the delivery. Lyon described the route as a "blind trail" and "nothing like a road." He soon became lost and never revealed if he finally found his way to Monistique.¹⁴

By the late 1860s Hutchins moved on to alternative pursuits, leaving delivery of the mail to others.¹⁵ Into this void entered Reuben Allen. Allen transported the mail by boat from Escanaba to Garden, and during the summer of 1868, his 15-year-old daughter Elizabeth carried the mail to Monistique on horseback over the Portage Trail.¹⁶

9   The Garden Peninsula Historical Society, *Our Heritage,* 1982, p. 15
10 Ibid., p. 194
11 *Escanaba Daily Press,* April 12, 1931, p. 13
12 "Portage Trail" *Escanaba Daily Press,* February 22, 1931, p.13
13 Ibid.
14 "Menominee Pioneer Tells About Early Day Mail Carrying" *Escanaba Daily Press,* December 30, 1933, p. 3
15 *Escanaba Daily Press,* February 22, 1931, p. 13
16 The Garden Peninsula Historical Society, *Our Heritage,* 1982, p. 194. See Also: *Escanaba Daily Press,* April 12, 1931, p. 13

Mail Was Brought here On Horseback in 1868 By Manistique Woman

By her neighbors she is known as "grandma," by the Indians she was called "the white queen;" and by the residents of the Garden peninsula she is referred to as the first white child to live in what is now the little fishing village of Garden. The subject of these appelations is a little white-haired old-lady, Mrs. Mike White, who is now spending the closing days of her epic career alone in a quaint little house close to the shores of Lake Michigan, the same body of water whose tempests she knew when she was but a demure maiden in her 'teens.

Her early life was filled with adventure such as the modern girl can only dream of, but never attain. Fate started her glorious career when she was born on a canal boat in Monroe county, Rochester, New York, on February 15, 1852. Soon after her birth her parents moved to Chicago where her father, Reuben Allen, was employed as a carpenter. Her mother was ill with typhoid and was advised to go north by physicians. Thus it happened that Elizabeth Allen was the first white child to live in Garden Bay, for her mother came to live with Mr. and Mrs. David Gray, Elizabeth's grandparents, who were the first white folks to locate in that vicinity. Six months later they were joined by Mr. Allen, who in his new environment, devoted his time to fishing and trading.

Lived in Wilderness

Elizabeth, at this time was only two years old. Here she grew up in a wilderness scarcely peopled by white people, living the crude hard life which is common to all pioneers who attempt to bring civilization into a new territory. When she grew older she used to go out on the lake with her father, help him pull in his trout-laden nets while standing on the stern of the little fishing smack, clad in cork soled shoes which prevented her from sliding off of the slippery deck.

The catch used to be salted away in barrels and half-barrels until some trading vessel would call to take them to Chicago where they would be sold on the market.

Later on Mr. Allen used his knowledge of carpentry by building a sailing vessel at Sac Bay and began trading provisions and clothing which he would purchase at Green Bay and sell in the various fishing ports along the shore of Lake Michigan at points such as Garden, Sac Bay, Mackinaw City, Escanaba, Beaver Island, Washington Harbor, etc. Elizabeth always accompanied him on these trips and soon came to know almost every mile of the shoreline from Green Bay to Mackinaw City. They encountered many

SOCIAL

Escanaba Daily Press, April 12, 1931, p. 13

Extending twelve and a half miles through a densely timbered wilderness, the trail ran north from Garden crossing Birch Creek, then east to Little Harbor and on to the future site of the village of Thompson. After passing near Barque Point, the trail wound around Indian Lake to the sawmill settlement of Epsport, at the mouth of the Monistique River. In many places the path was just wide enough to permit a single horse and rider to squeeze through.[17] Young Elizabeth was stuck by the trail's awesome beauty, especially in the plains where majestic forests of virgin eastern white pine and tamarack completely enveloped her.[18]

On her return home, Elizabeth forded the Indian River and stopped by the Ojibwa Indian village on the shores of Indian Lake. Here she rested

17 *Escanaba Daily Press,* February 22, 1931, p. 13
18 *Escanaba Daily Press,* April 12, 1931, p. 13

and partook in a meal. The tribe's elderly chief, Antoine Ossawinamakee, became quite fond of Elizabeth, with her long brown curls and adventuresome spirit. He referred to her as the "white queen." Elizabeth continued her weekly mail deliveries throughout the summer of 1868. The following winter, mail service to Monistique was accomplished by a Native American who mushed over the snow with a dogsled team.[19]

When a retrospective item appeared in the local newspaper in September of 1933 telling of Elizabeth Allen's exploits carrying the mail during the summer of 1868, two prominent Civil War veterans scoffed at the idea. James Lyon and Henri Brassel both labeled the story as fiction.[20] Those two distinguished veterans could be excused for not recalling an event which took place sixty-five years previously. They remembered Harry Hutchins who undoubtedly socialized freely with the fishermen at Garden and the lumbermen at Monistique. A young girl riding alone through a remote wilderness would have been much more discreet. So, Elizabeth spent the summer of 1868 communing with the aged Ojibwa Indian chief while sharing a meal.

Elizabeth's life took a dramatic turn in the autumn of 1868. In September of that year she married John Stark in a ceremony before a Justice of the Peace at Sac Bay.[21] Stark, age 32, had emigrated from Germany before serving with the 16th Illinois Cavalry during the Civil War. Self employed as a cooper, the future looked bright for Stark and his young bride.

The couple soon moved to St. Martins Island in northern Lake Michigan. Within a few years, Elizabeth had given birth to several children which led to conflicts in her marriage. Stark became increasingly resentful of the cost of providing for his growing family. By 1880, the Starks had moved to the village of Thompson but the marital discord only increased. Stark drank and became violent at times, striking and choking Elizabeth. She was to lose four of her fourteen children along the way, including a son, Reuben, named after her father. Then in March of 1888 Stark deserted the family altogether—refusing to provide any support for his wife or his eleven surviving children.[22] Elizabeth was forced to provide for her children alone. Exhibiting the grit and determination that had sustained her in the

---

19   Ibid.
20   *Escanaba Daily Press,* December 30, 1933, p. 1. See Also: "Pioneer, 90, Writes Of Manistique To Garden Mail Route" *Escanaba Daily Press,* January 4, 1934, p. 5.
21   Schoolcraft County Circuit Court Archives, Margaret E. Stark v. John Stark, Bill of Complaint, November 3, 1893.
22   Ibid.

past, Elizabeth performed hard physical labor to ensure that her little ones were clothed, educated and properly fed. Despite all the hardships, she somehow persevered.[23] Elizabeth filed for divorce in November of 1893.

Finally, free from her first husband, Elizabeth married for a second time on September 22, 1894. John Phenes was a bachelor who had served with the 153rd New York Infantry during the Civil War. He owned a farm in Thompson and welcomed Elizabeth and her five remaining minor children into his home. The marriage appears to have been a happy one, lasting until his death in January of 1907. Elizabeth's third husband was Michael White who passed away in 1919.

Elizabeth (who by then was known as Grandma White) lived the remainder of her life alone in her home in Manistique, a short distance from Lake Michigan. In her later years she took up smoking a corn cob pipe, which she said relaxed her.[24] She died in August of 1934 at the age of 81. Hailed as a "highly respected pioneer," she left a legacy of courage, adventure and devotion to family. Her life was an exemplar of the unheralded role which women played in settling the untamed frontier.

The grave of Margaret Elizabeth Allen White, Lakeview Cemetery, Manistique, Michigan.

---

23 Schoolcraft County Circuit Court Archives, Margaret E. Stark v. John Stark, Affidavits of Witnesses, 1893,
24 "Garden Woman, 81, Smokes Pipe" *Escanaba Daily Press,* September 19, 1933, p. 5.

Chapter Ten:
The Last Log Drive

A log drive on the Driggs River in Schoolcraft County. Schoolcraft County Historical Society, Photo, G. Leslie Bouchour Collection

In July of 1929, the largest remaining stand of Michigan's virgin white pine forest floated down the winding Manistique River toward the Stack Lumber Company sawmill in the town of Manistique. The giant pine had been scattered over 3,200 acres of swampy forest at the head of the Driggs River, a tributary of the Manistique River—in an area previously considered too inaccessible for logging operations.[1] The 1929 drive included 600,000 feet of Norway and white pine, 1,000,000 feet of hemlock and 800,000 feet of hardwood (birch, oak, maple, elm and basswood).[2] The log drive marked the end of big pine lumbering in Michigan which began along the Saginaw River valley in 1833. Once thought inexhaustible, the great

1   "Michigan's Last Pine Log Drive In This County" *Manistique Pioneer Tribune,* Manistique, Michigan, July 5, 1929, p.1 and P.8.
2   Ibid.

pine forests were all logged off in Lower Michigan by 1895 and in Upper Michigan by 1905. A total of 190 billion feet of lumber had succumbed to the woodman's axe.[3]

Frank Cookson, Manistique Centennial booklet, 1960.

The 1929 drive paled in comparison to those of the 1880s and 1890s, when 100 million to 125 million feet of virgin pine logs floated down the Manistique River each year. It is estimated that over 3 billion feet of pine lumber was driven down the Manistique from the time that lumbering operations began in the area in the early 1850s.[4]

Pioneer lumberman, Frank N. Cookson, was in charge of this final drive of the white pine era. Cookson was born in Greenfield, Maine, in February of 1863. He began working in the woods at the age of 14 and by the time he was 20 had held jobs in almost every facet of big pine lumbering.[5] Cookson came to Upper Michigan in 1888 joining his older brother Edwin who had arrived in 1875. Frank initially worked in his brother's lumber camp. By the early 1890's, Frank was hired as foreman of the river drive on the East Branch of the Fox River in Schoolcraft County.[6] Cookson soon gained the reputation as one of the Chicago Lumbering Company's most capable camp foremen and expert river drivers. Cookson operated lumber camps and was in charge of river drives for nearly 40 consecutive years thereafter.[7]

Harvey Saunders, a nephew of Cookson and a Maine logging veteran, was foreman for the drive on the Manistique River in 1929. Saunders was born in May of 1878 in Greenfield, Maine. Harvey was just two years old when his father died in a tragic accident, so he and his mother went to live with his grandparents, Joseph and Maria Cookson. The Cookson

3   Ibid.
4   Ibid.
5   "Frank N. Cookson Passes Suddenly Result Of Stroke" *Manistique Pioneer Tribune,* Manistique, Michigan, January 21, 1932. p.1
6   "Autobiography" Harvey C. Saunders papers, Michigan State University Archives and Historical Collections, East Lansing, Michigan
7   "Michigan's Last Pine Log Drive Now Going Down Manistique River" *Escanaba Daily Press,* Escanaba, Michigan, June 23, 1929, p. 11.

family included five boys and three girls. When Harvey was just seven years old, his uncles—woodsmen all—fitted him with a pair of caulked boots and began teaching him the skills of a river driver. He later honed his specialized talents on Maine's great Penobscot River, before coming to Upper Michigan in 1898.[8]

Logs were piled on a banking ground similar to the one pictured above at Hovey, to await the spring log drive. Schoolcraft County Historical Society photo.

The giant pine logs for the 1929 drive were harvested in the fall of 1928 in swampy ground at the head of the Driggs River in Schoolcraft County. These marvelous examples of white and Norway pine measured from 24 to 30 inches at the stump and stood between 90 and 110 feet high.[9] During the winter, the big timber was hauled to the banks of the river by drays and teams of horses, where it was piled on the skidways to await the spring driving season.

The historic drive began in April of 1929. The first step in any river drive was to clear the stream of debris. Any obstructions in the river during the drive could cause the logs to jam. A team of men with saws, axes and dynamite inspected the river and removed any stumps or trees that had fallen in since the previous year's drive. Once the stream was clear, the

---

8 "Autobiography" Harvey C. Saunders papers, Michigan State University Archives and Historical Collections, East Lansing, Michigan
9 *Escanaba Daily Press,* Escanaba, Michigan, June 23, 1929, p. 11.

drive could begin.[10]

Driving logs on the Driggs River was dependent on the use of dams to regulate the water level so the logs could be easily floated downstream. There were two dams on the Driggs River, the Ross Lake dam and the Driggs Lake dam. The Ross Lake dam was used primarily as a reservoir to hold the Driggs Lake dam up to an optimum level.[11]

At daybreak, the Driggs Lake dam was opened to begin the flood. The dam would remain open for approximately seven hours each day. Once the flood waters reached the rollways, the logs could be pulled from the river banks into the fast moving current below. Teams of horses with hook and lines pulled the logs from the center of the banking grounds to where they were rolled into the stream.[12]

Cookson employed about 100 men in his lumbering operations in 1929,[13] but only men with very specialized skills were river drivers. Clad in warm woolen clothing and wearing caulked boots,[14] the river drivers rode the logs downstream. They carried peaveys (long wooden poles with a metal hook on the end) to manipulate the logs and avoid pile-ups. The most dangerous aspect of a river driver's occupation was dislodging big jams. If a jam did occur, it was the river driver's job to find the log that was causing the jam and free it from any snag or debris. Once the offending log was located and dislodged, the river men scampered to the safety of the shore. During the heyday of big pine lumbering, many river drivers lost their lives when they were swept away by the raging cascade of wood and water.[15] For large or intractable jams, dynamite was used to clear the obstruction and get the timber moving again.

The pine and hemlock for the 1929 drive were floated a distance of 30 miles on the Driggs to where it joins the larger Manistique River. Here the logs were held in a boom until the spring flood on the Manistique had receded and the water no longer overflowed its banks.

---

10 "Autobiography" Harvey C. Saunders papers, Michigan State University Archives and Historical Collections, East Lansing, Michigan, pp. 3-4.
11 Ibid. p.2
12 Ibid. p.4
13 'Logging Now Near Close" *Escanaba Daily Press,* Escanaba, Michigan, March 13, 1929, p.7
14 Caulked boots had sharp metal studs embedded in the soles to provide better traction while riding logs downstream.
15 *Escanaba Daily Press,* Escanaba, Michigan, June 23, 1929, p.11

River Hogs on the Manistique River, Schoolcraft County Historical Society photo, G. Leslie Bouchour Collection

When the flood waters subsided, the hemlock logs were sent down the river first. Hemlock logs float well but are not buoyant enough to support hardwood, so they are unsuitable for rafts. Once the hemlock logs were on their way, the pine was allowed to float down the horseshoe curves of the Manistique for a distance of ten miles. At this point, a boom constructed with logs linked end to end by strong chains was stretched across the river in the middle of horseshoe bend. The logs were thus directed against the riverbank where they were held.[16]

During the winter, hardwood timber had been piled along the shore of the river to be ferried to Manistique in rafts composed of pine logs and hardwood. Otherwise, the maple, oak and other hardwood species would sink to the bottom. After each raft was finished it would be sent on through the boom to the Stack Lumber Company mill in Manistique. Saunders and his crew were able to construct approximately seventy-five rafts each day.[17] The whole rafting enterprise (lasting three weeks) was finished in mid-July, 1929.

Saunders required only six river drivers to complete the final phase of the 1929 operation. A cook's raft called a Wanigan, followed closely behind the drive. It was crudely constructed and topped off with a tar paper shack. A stovepipe could be seen protruding through the roof. The

16 Ibid.
17 "Last Drive Is At Manistique" *Escanaba Daily Press,* Escanaba, Michigan, July 26, 1929, p.8

Wanigan housed the chef's stove and sleeping quarters for the men. Ed Fountain was the chef for the 1929 drive.[18] The river men were always well fed during the drive. Ham and eggs were served on the Wanigan as opposed to sowbelly and corned beef, which was the normal fare in the lumber camps.[19]

Once all the pine and hardwood rafts had reached Manistique, the "short-stuff" including cedar posts and pulpwood was sent down the river. By August of 1929, the legendary era of virgin pine lumbering had come to a close.

Frank Cookson's life-span closely paralleled that momentous epoch. Born in Maine in 1863, Cookson died unexpectedly in January of 1932.[20] His nephew, Harvey Saunders went on to be employed with the Department of the Interior in 1938, working at the Seney National Wildlife Refuge until his retirement in 1956. Saunders died in 1967 at age 88.[21]

---

18 Ibid.
19 *Lumberjack, Inside An Era in the Upper Peninsula of Michigan,* William S. Crowe, 2002 Lynn McGlothlin Emerick and Ann McGlothlin Weller, p.44
20 *Manistique Pioneer Tribune,* Manistique, Michigan, January 21, 1932. p.1
21 *Lumberjack, Inside An Era in the Upper Peninsula of Michigan,* William S. Crowe, p.45

Chapter Eleven:
The Jamestown Lumbering Settlement

A mile north of present-day Manistique, on the river of the same name, there once stood a bustling sawmill settlement known as Jamestown. Its founders were men of industry, who were undaunted by the enormous task of creating a thriving lumbering community in the heart of a dense wilderness. Natural calamities and poor geography doomed their efforts and today there is no trace of the community that once existed there.

Ebenezer James was born in Philadelphia on March 4, 1836 to Ebenezer and Mary James. The James's were devout Quakers and young Ebenezer was reared in the traditions of that faith.[1] James was described by his friends as a "most companionable man" who loved to engage in long conversations about philosophy, religion and politics.[2] In 1854, he came west to Oshkosh, Wisconsin where he married Mary Fletcher on December 29, 1858.[3] Eight children were born to this union, including seven daughters and one son.[4]

Shortly after his arrival in Oshkosh, James entered the lumbering manufacturing business. His first sawmill burned to the ground after only a year in operation but was rebuilt in 1857, in partnership with August Stille. The firm of James & Stille prospered for nearly two decades, until this mill too was destroyed in the great Oshkosh fire of 1875.[5]

The Oshkosh mill was never rebuilt as James had decided to pursue lumbering opportunities in upper Michigan. Three years earlier, in 1872, James, along with Dougald McMillen, purchased 5,000 acres of pine

[1] "E. James Is No More" *Oshkosh Daily Northwestern,* Oshkosh, Wisconsin, February 13, 1912, p.1
[2] *Reminiscences,* Emory Fiske Skinner, 1908, Vestal Printing Co., Chicago, Illinois, p. 46
[3] *Oshkosh Daily Northwestern,* Oshkosh, Wisconsin, February 13, 1912, p.1
[4] "Death of Mrs. James" *Oshkosh Daily Northwestern,* Oshkosh, Wisconsin, May 21, 1885
[5] "For Humanity's Sake" *Oshkosh Daily Northwestern,* Oshkosh, Wisconsin, November 14, 1908, p.8

timber land north of what was then known as "Monistique" on the northern shore of Lake Michigan in the Upper Peninsula.[6] James and his former partner, August Stille, purchased 5,000 additional acres sometime prior to 1875.[7]

The James & Ruggles sawmill at Jamestown. Photo courtesy Schoolcraft County Historical Society

In 1876, following the destruction of his mill in Oshkosh, Ebenezer James with his brother William and fellow Oshkosh lumberman Constant Ruggles, came north to Monistique to oversee the construction of the new James & Ruggles sawmill. Once they arrived in Monistique, the men soon discovered that the Chicago Lumbering Company owned almost the entire town including all the land on both sides of the Monistique River near the harbor. Consequently, the three men had to look elsewhere to build their new sawmill.[8] About a mile up the river they came upon some unclaimed low-lying government land, timbered primarily with tamarack and cedar. The location was far from ideal, but there were few other suitable options. Ebenezer James put in his claim at the land office and construction of the mill began soon thereafter.[9]

The new mill would be steam powered and its erection was an enormous undertaking. The low ground was cleared and corduroy roads constructed.

---

6   "Wisconsin" *The Milwaukee Sentinel,* Milwaukee, Wisconsin, November 16, 1872
7   "Important Decision" *Oshkosh Daily Northwestern,* Oshkosh, Wisconsin, September 14, 1880
8   "Jamestown" Harvey C. Saunders papers, Michigan State University Archives and Historical Collections, East Lansing, Michigan, p.1
9   Ibid.

All the building materials for the mill including the boilers and smokestacks had to be brought in by boat, and hauled to the building site by wagons and teams of horses.[10]

Pioneer lumberman Edwin Cookson, Photo courtesy Anthony Perkins.

Advertisements in the Oshkosh newspapers encouraged men to come north for jobs in the new James and Ruggles mill. Out of necessity, the boarding house was the first building erected at the Jamestown location. Pioneer lumbermen Edwin Cookson and Murdock McNeil saw the ads in the Oshkosh papers and were among the first arrivals. They came and made their homes here. Before long, a flourishing settlement could be seen along the bank of the Monistique River, on what earlier had been considered worthless swamp land.

The enterprise prospered at the start. The company's pine timber located north of Monistique in Hiawatha Township could easily be floated down the Monistique River to the Jamestown mill. A wooden, elevated tramway for a horse drawn railway was built to transport the finished lumber from the mill to the harbor where it could be shipped to market. The future seemed bright, but it was only an illusion.

The first in a series of misfortunes took place near the end of July, 1877. Ebenezer James's son Willie and two other boys were bathing in the Monistique River near the sawmill. One of the boys, Georgie Choate, a friend of Willie's from Oshkosh, fell into a hole and disappeared. The two other boys tried to rescue him, but were unable to do so without possibly

10 "Jamestown" Harvey C. Saunders papers, Michigan State University Archives and Historical Collections, East Lansing, Michigan, p.2

drowning themselves. Willie was forced to let go of his panicked friend and run to the mill for help. The men flocked to the shore. They dove down in all directions, but it was an hour before Georgie's body was finally found. Ebenezer James accompanied the boy's body back to Oshkosh and broke the sad news to his stricken parents. The funeral was conducted from James' home.[11]

Misfortune of a different kind visited Jamestown the following year. The summer of 1878 had been tinder dry. The fire danger was extreme, especially since cut over pine land provides excellent fuel for combustion. Any spark or lightening strike could ignite an inferno. Those fears were realized during the first week of August when a wildfire came from the woods and threatened to destroy the entire lumbering settlement. The barn, ice house and a large quantity of lumber were consumed by the flames. A half mile of the wooden railway was also burned, along with the elevated platform adjoining the mill. The men concentrated their efforts on saving the mill itself, which was spared only through tremendous exertion. Total damages were estimated at $5000, and were not covered by insurance.[12]

The fire damages, though costly, could be overcome. However, the mills location proved to be its Achilles heel. Once the pine land north of the mill near the Monistique River was depleted, it became increasingly difficult to keep the Jamestown mill supplied with logs.

James's remaining stand of pine timber was located on Murphy Creek near Thunder Lake. The logs cut from this timber had to be brought to the Jamestown mill by a cumbersome and circuitous route. The logs were first floated across Indian Lake and down the Indian River to where it meets the Monistique River. From there, they were rafted or placed in a boom and towed upstream on the Monistique to the James Brothers mill. James used a sidewheel steamboat to tow his logs upstream. A power wench was located on the stern of the boat along with a 25 foot pole called a grouser. A heavy rope was attached from the wench to the raft of logs. The grouser was lowered on end to the bottom of the stream to hold the steamboat in place while the raft was being pulled forward by the wench. Once the raft was near the stern of the steamboat it was unhooked from the wench and secured in the river by ropes tied to trees along the riverbank. The grouser was lifted up from the river bottom allowing the steamer to sail a

---

[11] "Drowning of Georgie Cholate" *Oshkosh Daily Northwestern,* Oshkosh, Wisconsin, July 31, 1877

[12] "Fire at Monastique" *Oshkosh Daily Northwestern,* Oshkosh, Wisconsin, August 7, 1878

little further upstream where the whole process was repeated until the raft finally reached the mill.[13]

This ingenious plan to supply the Jamestown mill with logs might have worked well if they were the only company using the river, but that was not the case. The Chicago Lumbering Company drove millions of board feet of timber down the Manistique River each year. In order to tow their logs upstream, the James & Ruggles men had to close off the river above their mill. This could be done for only short periods at a time, as they lacked a facility for temporarily storing the Chicago Lumbering Company's logs. In addition, the labor cost to close off the river was prohibitive. The location of the Chicago Lumbering Company's sorting piers three fourths of a mile downstream from the Jamestown mill was another obstacle. There were so many Chicago Lumbering Company logs coming downstream, that they literally filled the river from the sorting piers upstream past the Jamestown mill. Ironically, the Jamestown mill stood idle for the lack of the raw material for the manufacture of lumber.[14]

By mutual agreement, the partnership between the James brothers and Constant Ruggles was dissolved in February of 1879.[15] Ruggles took his share of the company, not in cash, but in a year's supply of food stuffs for himself and his family. Ruggles focused his efforts toward improving his homestead east of Manistique. He began clearing the land and cutting the timber into cordwood, which he delivered to the dock in Manistique where it was sold as fuel for visiting wood burning steamboats.[16] Ruggles remained in Manistique for nearly 20 years, engaging in numerous successful business ventures.

The James Brother's mill remained in operation through the summer of 1883, but without a reliable supply of logs, the losses mounted. James sold the remaining assets of the company, including the logs and standing timber to the Chicago Lumbering Company. That firm also employed many of the men who had formerly worked at the Jamestown mill. In June of 1885, the editor of the *Semi-Weekly Pioneer,* commented on the dramatic decline of the once bustling community.

13 "Jamestown" Harvey C. Saunders papers, Michigan State University Archives and Historical Collections, East Lansing, Michigan, p.2
14 "Jamestown" Harvey C. Saunders papers, Michigan State University Archives and Historical Collections, East Lansing, Michigan, p.3
15 "Dissolution" *Oshkosh Daily Northwestern,* Oshkosh, Wisconsin, February 13, 1879
16 "Jamestown" Harvey C. Saunders papers, Michigan State University Archives and Historical Collections, East Lansing, Michigan, p.3

"Jamestown now is almost a deserted village; we believe there is only one family living there now."[17]

Ebenezer James returned to Oshkosh, but was never again engaged in the lumber manufacturing business. Instead, he formed a partnership in a company that produced pumps, and later owned a wholesale paper distributorship. In 1885, his wife Mary died unexpectedly at age 47 following a brief illness.[18] He never remarried.

In his later life, James served several years as President of the Winnebago County Humane Society, which sought to prevent cruelty to both people and animals. He described his time spent on behalf of the humane society as both "a pleasure and a duty."[19] Ebenezer James died in Oshkosh on March 4, 1912, just one month short of his 84th birthday.

---

17 *Semi-Weekly Pioneer,* Manistique, Michigan, June 6, 1885, p.1
18 Death of Mrs. James" *Oshkosh Daily Northwestern,* Oshkosh, Wisconsin, May 21, 1885
19 "For Humanity's Sake" *Oshkosh Daily Northwestern,* Oshkosh, Wisconsin, November 14, 1908, p.8

Chapter Twelve:
The Voyage of the Griffin

Woodcut of the legendary *Griffin*, courtesy Wikimedia Commons

No one knows how the Griffin perished or where she now lies. Celebrated as the first sailing ship to navigate the Great Lakes, the Griffin left Washington Island in northern Lake Michigan on September 18, 1679.[1] Its intended port of call was the great falls at Niagara, where it was to deliver a cargo of beaver pelts and furs—but the Griffin never arrived. The renowned vessel was built by order of the French explorer, Rene-Robert Cavalier, Sieur de LaSalle, under the wary and prying eyes of the Seneca warriors, who threatened to burn the ship before it could ever be set afloat.[2] Though not completely finished, the bark was launched from the

---

[1] Father Louis Hennepin *Description of Louisiana*, Translated from the Edition of 1683, by John Gilmay Shea, New York, 1880 p. 106.
[2] Ibid. p. 84; See Also: Francis Parkman, *LaSalle and the Discovery of the Great West, Vol. I,* Boston: Little Brown, and Co., New York: J. F. Taylor and Co. 1897, p.147

vicinity of Niagara Falls in March of 1679. Her sailing career lasted less than a year, but the search for clues concerning her fateful final journey has spanned centuries.

A mythological animal of enormous strength and courage, the Griffin was said to be the guardian of great treasure and a protector of the divine. The creature was endowed with the body and tail of a lion, and the head and wings of an eagle with eagle's talons on its front feet. LaSalle named his bark the Griffin to honor the governor of New France, Count de Frontenac, whose coat of arms featured the fearless beast. LaSalle often said that "he wished to see the Griffin soar above the crows" which referred to Frontenac's political rivalry with the Jesuits.[3] LaSalle's Griffin was a two-masted, square rigged bark, approximately 50 to 60 feet in length, with a cargo capacity of 45 tuns (barrels).[4] The carved likeness of a griffin with outstretched wings adorned her prow. Five menacing cannon stood guard, peering out through the ship's portholes.[5]

After its launch, LaSalle's men sailed the Griffin up the Niagara River, securely mooring the bark at Black Rock, where they completed work on her construction. Here, the men also awaited the return of their commander, LaSalle. He brought with him the Griffin's anchor and cables, salvaged from the wreck of his supply ship, which had been lost the previous December.[6] On August 7, 1679, LaSalle's Griffin proceeded upstream to the mouth of the Niagara River, and entered Lake Erie. This great inland lake had never before been crossed by a ship with sails.[7] Three days later the Griffin entered the Strait of Detroit. The crew marveled at the lush prairies, bordered by forests and dotted with groves of walnut, chestnut and oak trees. There was abundant wildlife too, including great herds of white-tail deer, bears and flocks of swans and other water fowl. The bulwarks of the Griffin were soon filled with the carcasses of wild game, including bears which the Franciscan Friar, Louis Hennepin described as "by no means fierce and very good to eat."[8] The men made wine from wild grapes, which was used in religious services.

[3] Hennepin, *Description of Louisiana*, p. 86. See Also: Parkman, *LaSalle and the Discovery of the Great West*, p. 149.
[4] Parkman, *LaSalle and the Discovery of the Great West*, p.148; See Also, "Detroiter May Have Located 'Ghost Ship', *The News Palladium*, Benton Harbor, Michigan, Oct. 24, 1969, p.1.
[5] Parkman, *LaSalle and the Discovery of the Great West*, p. 149
[6] Ibid. *p.149-150*
[7] Hennepin, *Description of Louisiana*, p. 90. See Also: Parkman, *LaSalle and the Discovery of the Great West*, p. 152
[8] Hennepin, *Description of Louisiana*, p. 92

LaSalle's brief respite of good fortune held as the Griffin sailed across Lake St. Clair and ventured into Lake Huron. The following day the Griffin was beset by calm winds which were an omen of the great storm to come. The storm came and steadily increased in intensity. The wind and waves tossed the intrepid ship about. In great peril and unable to find shelter from the gale, LaSalle "commended his enterprise to God." In a prayer to St. Anthony, LaSalle promised to build a chapel in honor of the Saint, if only the Griffin could be delivered from the storm.[9]

Woodcut of Rene-Robert Cavallier LaSalle, Courtesy Wikimedia Commons

The gale force winds finally abated, enabling the Griffin to reach safe harbor behind the point at St. Ignace near Michilimackinac on present day Mackinac Island. They arrived here on August 27, 1679 and fired their cannon, which both surprised and frightened the native citizens.[10] The straits area was home to Jesuit missionaries, French fur traders and bands of Huron and Ottawa Indians. Michilimackinac and its neighbor to the north, Sault Sainte Marie, were two of the most important gateways for northern and western Indian tribes, making their way each year to Montreal to trade their furs for French beads, axes, and other goods.[11]

The native tribes at Michilimackinac were fishermen, who used nets to harvest the plentiful whitefish and lake trout found in the waters off the

9 Ibid. pp. 95-96
10 Ibid. pp. 97, 99
11 Ibid. p. 102

strait. They also raised corn which provided year around sustenance.¹² The Hurons, who were well armed, gave LaSalle and his men an honorary salute by firing three volleys with their rifles. Though outwardly supportive of LaSalle, the Indians were mistrustful of his motives and fearful of his floating fortress.¹³

Franciscan Friar Louis Hennepin,
Image courtesy Wikimedia Commons

Among the Frenchmen at St. Ignace, there were traders who both feared and despised LaSalle and sought to poison his relationship with the Indians. LaSalle, in the license of discovery granted to him by the king, was forbidden to trade with the Ottawa and other western tribes who yearly journeyed to Montreal with their furs. The French traders at St. Ignace were jealous of LaSalle's relationship with Count de Frontenac, who was the governor of New France. They believed that regardless of the king's prohibition, the governor would sustain LaSalle in his illicit trade with the Ottawa and other tribes.¹⁴ Hence, they tried to undermine LaSalle's expedition by discouraging and demoralizing members of his crew. During the fall of 1678, in advance of his expedition, LaSalle had dispatched 15 men with canoes and trade goods to be used with the Indians in Illinois. At Michilimackinac, LaSalle was informed that many of these men had lost faith, and had become convinced that their undertaking would end in disaster. Six had deserted and took a large share of the trade goods for themselves. Four of these men were found at Michilimackinac and were arrested. Two others were taken into custody at Sault Sainte Marie, and some of the stolen trade goods recovered.¹⁵

On September 2, 1679, the Griffin departed St. Ignace, sailing westward into northern Lake Michigan, arriving finally at one of the islands off Green

12 Ibid. pp. 99-101
13 Ibid. p. 100
14 Parkman, *LaSalle and the Discovery of the Great West,* pp. 153-154
15 Parkman, *LaSalle and the Discovery of the Great West,* pp. 154-155; See Also: Hennepin, *Description of Louisiana,* pp. 103-104

Bay.[16] Here, LaSalle was met by truly friendly natives. In a show of good will, the chief of the Pottawattamie nation rowed his canoe out to greet the Griffin and was welcomed aboard ship. He presented LaSalle with a peace pipe, called a calumet. The bowl of the pipe was made of polished red stone and its long stem was highly embellished and adorned with hair and feathers. The calumet was smoked to seal any important agreement, and was especially important in concluding treaties with neighboring tribes. The sacred emblem would prove to be a dependable key to safe passage when LaSalle and his men encountered the Illinois Indians who lived along the southern shore of Lake Michigan, and who were allied with the Pottawattamie against the Iroquois. The natives respected the spirit of peace embodied in the calumet. Any violation of that trust would bring about their own destruction.[17]

In another turn of good fortune, LaSalle was reunited with several steadfast members of his advance party who had collected a large cache of furs.[18] Although LaSalle's journey of exploration had been sanctioned by the king, LaSalle was left to fund the expedition himself.[19] As a result, he had borrowed heavily and these debts weighed upon him. Motivated by a desire to satisfy his creditors, LaSalle made an impulsive and ill-advised decision which crippled his future prospects for success. He ordered the furs loaded aboard the Griffin and sent the ship, with a crew of six, back to Niagara. The precious cargo was to be delivered as payment to his benefactors. Once delivered, the bark was to return to Michilimackinac and await further instructions. But the Griffin also carried trade merchandise, tools and other supplies that were vital to his mission.[20] By sending the Griffin to Niagara, he also lost the military advantage of the arms aboard the bark, which could be used to defend his party against a hostile Indian attack. Instead, LaSalle trusted all to the pilot who had incompetently wrecked his supply ship the previous December.

The Griffin left Washington Island on September 18, 1679, sailing in an easterly direction with a favorable light west wind. Once the bark disappeared from sight, it never was seen or heard from again. The most likely scenario is that the ship foundered in a storm somewhere in the waters of northern Lake Michigan. Others have speculated that the

---

16   Hennepin, *Description of Louisiana*, p. 104
17   Ibid. pp. 112-113
18   Ibid. p.104, See Also: Parkman, *LaSalle and the Discovery of the Great West*, .p 156
19   Parkman, *LaSalle and the Discovery of the Great West*, p. 125
20   Hennepin, *Description of Louisiana*, p.105

Ottawa or Pottawattamie Indians, acting out of fear and jealousy, may have boarded the ship, killed the crew and set the vessel on fire. LaSalle became convinced that the Griffin had been scuttled by his own men, who then made off with its valuable cargo of furs.

It wasn't until the following day, September 19, 1679, that LaSalle left Green Bay to continue his expedition. The Cavalier was intent on finding a water route from the Great Lakes to the Mississippi River. He set out with the remainder of his crew, traveling along the lakeshore in four canoes headed to Illinois. Friar Louis Hennepin was in one of the canoes and wrote an account of the terrifying storm which arose soon after their departure:

> "We took our course southerly towards the mainland four good leagues distant from the island of the [Pottawattamie]. In the middle of the traverse and amid the most beautiful calm in the world, a storm arose which endangered our lives, and which made us fear for the bark, and more for ourselves. We completed this great passage amid the darkness of night, calling to one another so as not to part company. The water often entered our canoes, and the impetuous wind lasted four days with a fury like the greatest tempests of ocean. We nevertheless reached the shore in a little sandy bay, and stayed five days waiting for the lake to grow calm."[21]

After enduring great hardships, on the first day of November, 1679, LaSalle arrived at the mouth of the St. Joseph River (which he called the Miami). To keep his men occupied, he ordered that they build a fort at the head of the river, where the city of St. Joseph, Michigan, now lies. LaSalle also dispatched two men up the eastern coast of Lake Michigan to Michilimackinac. They were to serve as guides to the pilot of the Griffin, who he hoped had arrived safely back from Niagara with his ship.[22]

Near the end of November, LaSalle's close associate, Henri de Tonty, arrived at Fort Miami from Michilimackinac with a party of men and two canoes filled with food and supplies. Tonty also brought disturbing news concerning the Griffin:

> ". . . our newcomers said that the bark had not touched at Michilimackinac, and that they had heard no tidings of her from the Indians, coming from all sides of the lakes, nor from

---

21 Ibid. pp. 108-109
22 Ibid. p. 133

the two men who had been sent to Michilimackinac and who they had met on the way. He [LaSalle] feared and with reason that his bark had been wrecked."[23]

So began the search for clues concerning the fate of the Griffin. LaSalle was convinced that the Griffin had been deliberately sunk by its pilot and crew, to cover up the theft of its precious cargo of furs. He claimed that he had discovered evidence of their treachery though his later contacts with the Indians. Historians however, have labeled those verbal reports as far from conclusive.[24]

During the past century, many have claimed to have found the Griffin, but irrefutable proof has been elusive. Reports surfaced in the 1930s, and later in the 1950s and 60s that the remains of the Griffin had been located near Manitoulin Island, in northern Lake Huron. In 1937, Eugene F. McDonald, skipper of the yacht *Mizpah,* discovered an ancient shipwreck in the waters off the western shore of Manitoulin Island. He described the wreck as being "of extra heavy construction" and "about the size of the Griffin." McDonald went on to explain that the part of the shipwreck that remained was "entirely hand hewn, and held together by huge iron spikes."[25] Along with an iron spike, McDonald salvaged a block of wood from the hull. Neither could be conclusively identified as coming from LaSalle's vessel.[26] The discovery of the Griffin's armaments including five cannons (two of brass) would greatly assist in authenticating any shipwreck as being the one built by LaSalle's men at Niagara Falls.

In September of 1955, the press reported the possible discovery of the Griffin in "a small cove on an island near Tobermory, [Ontario], at the tip of the western arm of land enclosing the Georgian Bay." Artifacts from the shipwreck were retrieved by Orrie Vail, a commercial fisherman living in Tobermory. The relics included pieces of a blackened hull and handmade iron bolts. Experts at the Royal Ontario Museum authenticated the type of ax marks on the hull as being between 200 and 300 years old.[27]

Five years later, in August of 1960, Norman McCready, who previously located the sunken Great Lakes freighter, *Carl Bradley,* announced that

23 Ibid. p. 134
24 Parkman, *LaSalle and the Discovery of the Great West,* p. 182
25 "Ancient Hull Is Discovered At Manitoulin", *The Evening News,* Sault Ste. Marie, Michigan, Sept. 2, 1937, p. 5
26 Ibid.
27 "Find Iron Bolts of Ancient Ship—First Built on Lakes", *The Sheboygan Press,* Sheboygan, Wisconsin, Sept. 29, 1955, p.1

he had salvaged timbers believed to be from the Griffin. The remnants of the shipwreck were located with the aid of underwater radar aboard McCready's cruiser *Penmanta*. Divers recovered a 20 foot plank, bolts and a section of the vessel's ribs in northern Lake Huron in the waters off Manitoulin Island.[28]

The most recent attempts to locate the Griffin have taken place near Fairport, on the southern tip of the Garden Peninsula, in northern Lake Michigan. Great Lakes shipwreck explorer Steve Libert believes that a wooden beam, first discovered in 2001, may have come from LaSalle's ship. The beam, which protruded from the lake bottom, was not attached to other wreckage as had been hoped. Nevertheless, French shipwreck experts who inspected the beam during the summer of 2013 believe that it may by a bowsprit similar in construction to those found on other ships of that era.[29] Carbon dating and samples of the wood have failed to establish beyond a doubt that the beam came from a 17th century vessel.[30] Skeptics speculate that the wooden beam was more likely an "abandoned fishing net stake."[31]

Ever confident, Libert continued his search for the shipwreck. He was rewarded during the summer of 2014 when his crew located a debris field 120 feet from where the wooden beam was discovered. Divers who examined the site found planks, pegs and nails similar to those of another of LaSalle's ships, the LaBelle, which sank in the Gulf of Mexico.[32] Further exploration is planned.

As for LaSalle, he eventually found his way to the Mississippi River via the Illinois and reached the Gulf of Mexico in August of 1682. There he claimed all the land watered by the Mississippi and its tributaries for Louis XIV, King of France. He named the territory Louisiana. LaSalle, who always demanded too much of his men, was killed by them in March of 1687 near the Brazos River in present day Texas. His murder followed a foolhardy attack against the Spanish in Mexico.

---

28 "Ruins Of Griffin Found In Huron", *The Herald Press,* St. Joseph, Michigan, Aug. 27, 1960, p. 1
29 "Griffin Shipwreck: Wooden Beam Not Attached To Buried Vessel, Researchers Say" John Flesher, *Associated Press*, June 13, 2013
30 "Lake Michigan researcher convinced he's found LaSalle's Griffin stateside", Michael Erskine, *Headline News,* July 9, 2014
31 Ibid.
32 "More evidence found that Griffin could be located in L. Michigan", Tom Sasvai, *Manitoulin West Recorder,* July 4, 2014

Chapter Thirteen:
Charles Ekberg, Pioneer Cobbler

Charles Ekberg was born in Skåne County in southern Sweden on April 30, 1862.[1] His early childhood was marked by hunger and deprivation. Charles was still an infant when his father was killed in a tragic accident that catapulted his family into poverty. Nine years later, his mother followed her husband to the grave. Heartbroken after his mother's death, Ekberg despaired for his future. The authorities planned to provide for the boy by sending him to reside with a humorless neighbor couple, where he would work for his room and board.[2]

When the day came for young Ekberg to be turned over to the custody of strangers, he vowed to run away. He was to begin his new life with the neighbor couple on Sweden's most celebrated holiday, Saint John's Day, which took place in midsummer. The festival presented the perfect opportunity for a small boy to disappear into the crowds. Left on his own for a time, Charles made his way to the depot. Unnoticed by the attendant at the station, Ekberg boarded an excursion train bound for Lund where he spent the day. When the celebration was concluded, the boy managed to sneak aboard a second train; this one headed for the seaport city of Malmö. While at the dock, he squeezed in among a crowd of travelers, boarding a ship bound for Copenhagen, Denmark.[3]

Tired and hungry, Ekberg wandered aimlessly for hours through the streets of Copenhagen, arriving finally in front of a market filled with fruits and vegetables. The shop owner noticed the boy staring yearningly at his produce, and he asked the boy if he wanted a job. The grocer fed the child and put him to work sorting potatoes and picking off the sprouts. A

---

[1] "Charles Ekberg Celebrates 90th Birthday Wednesday" *Escanaba Daily Press*, Escanaba, Michigan; May 1, 1952 p.14
[2] "Grampa Ekberg, 94, Recalls Early Days in Sweden and in Manistique" *Escanaba Daily Press*, May 6, 1955 p.8 Article by James Lowell
[3] Ibid.

bed was provided in the attic of the grocer's home. Before long, Ekberg earned enough money to buy his first pair of leather shoes and some new clothes.[4]

Charles Ekberg in his cobbler shop, circa 1948. Photo courtesy Schoolcraft County Historical Society

Charles worked hard and had an outgoing personality. The grocer looked after him until he found him a steady job as a cabin boy on a steam boat sailing between Copenhagen, Denmark and Hull, England. The ship's captain took young Ekberg under his wing, and taught him to read and write. He also schooled him in proper manners.

After working four years as a cabin boy, the captain arranged for the lad to be apprenticed as an iron worker on condition that he complete his neglected religious education by learning the Lutheran Catechism and being confirmed. Ekberg fulfilled his promise to the captain and was confirmed, but an accident at the foundry left his vision so impaired that he was forced to learn a new trade. By the time Ekberg reached the age of 17 he had completed an apprenticeship with a shoemaker and was dreaming

4   Ibid.

about what life could be like in America!⁵

The passage to America cost him nearly all of his savings from his work as a journeyman shoemaker. He arrived in New York during the spring of 1880 with $1.80 in his pocket. Job recruiters came daily to the port of entry, and Ekberg soon found himself riding in a boxcar with a group of other immigrants bound for Tonawanda, New York.

Tonawanda, New York was located on the shore of Lake Erie, where three masted schooners unloaded their cargos of pine and hardwood lumber from the forests of the Great Lakes region. Upon his arrival at the Weston Lumber Company in Tonawanda, Ekberg was assigned to work with a soft spoken, unassuming gentleman who liked to whittle. With a wagon and team of horses, the two men went about setting up the framework for lumber piles. Each set of timbers would be carefully leveled off and secured before moving on to the next. As the days wore on Ekberg would often see the man he had worked with on that first day. He would sit quietly at the dock turning a stick of wood into shavings, while other workers scurried all around him.⁶

Abijah Weston, President of the Chicago Lumbering Co., SCHS photo.

One day while unloading a schooner from a lumber mill in Michigan, Ekberg heard about the town of Manistique, where there was a large Scandinavian community and plenty of jobs in the mills. Ekberg determined that he would go there. He arrived in Manistique on June 29, 1880 and was assigned a job as a common laborer in the lumber yard. One day while working in the harbor, he spied his friend the whittler disembarking a schooner from Tonawanda. It was only then that Ekberg discovered who his soft-spoken friend actually was; Abijah Weston, owner of the

5   Ibid.
6   Ibid.

Chicago Lumbering Company.[7]

Ekberg stayed in Manistique for only a short time before his urge to wander became too much for him to resist. He made his way first to Escanaba where he worked at the ore docks using "pike poles" to shove iron ore into the holds of ships. Describing the foreman, who yelled and cursed constantly, as a "slave driver," he moved on to Menominee—and eventually made his way to Chicago. He was employed there as a bricklayer's helper prior to finding a job more in line with his training in a shoe store.[8] All the while he was in Chicago, his thoughts took him back to Manistique where he longed to return.

After he had saved $110 from his job in the shoe store, he purchased a supply of leather, a stitching machine, shoemaker's tools and passage on a boat to Fayette, Michigan. When he arrived at Fayette, he arranged for his supply of leather and tools to be placed on the stage to Manistique the following day. Not having enough money to purchase a ticket for himself he hiked across country to Manistique, slogging through the wet snow of early spring.

Ekberg met with the superintendent of the lumber mill, Martin Henderson Quick, and secured credit to purchase the lumber required to erect a store building. The lumber company bosses owned all of the property in Manistique, and they assigned him a location on Chippewa Avenue where he could build and open his business.[9] Ekberg made and repaired shoes in Manistique for over 60 years, working well into his 90's. In the early days the majority of his business consisted of work shoes for lumber jacks and mill hands. But he also made dress shoes for both men and women. When interviewed by a reporter for his 94th birthday in 1955, Ekberg showed off a pair of lady's shoes he had made 60 years earlier. They were very sharply pointed at the toe and 14 inches high.

Ekberg maintained a relationship with Abijah Weston for several years after he opened his store. Weston would stop into his shoe shop and visit—sometimes for hours. After he left, Ekberg would sweep up nearly a bushel of shavings off the floor, as Weston whittled all the while he talked.

7   Ibid.
8   Ibid.
9   Ibid.

Charles Ekberg at age 94. Photo courtesy Schoolcraft County Historical Society, Fish Family Collection

Charles Ekberg married Hanna Peterson in Manistique on February 25, 1885. The couple had four children. Hanna died first in November of 1924 at age 59. Her husband survived her by more than three decades. Ekberg's cobbler shop tools and equipment were donated to the Schoolcraft County Historical Society by the Fish family and are on permanent display.

Chapter Fourteen:
The Circuit Rider

Thomas J. MacMurray, Photo from his book *After Hours*, Courtesy Google Books

He traveled alone on horseback, riding for miles through an uninhabited wilderness before coming at last to a tiny hamlet. While there, he conducted religious services, visited the sick, buried the dead, comforted the grieving, joined couples in marriage and baptized the faithful uninitiated. The names and exploits of many of these frontier clergymen have faded into obscurity with the passage of time. But the Methodist circuit rider who visited Manistique left a legacy that endures to this day.

Born in Paisley, Scotland on July 23, 1852, Thomas J. MacMurray immigrated to Nova Scotia, Canada with his family in 1862[1]. As a young man he studied theology at Victoria College in Cobourg, Ontario, which served as a Methodist seminary. Soon after completing his studies he immigrated to Wisconsin where he began his life as a traveling minister.[2]

MacMurray arrived in Manistique during the mid-1870s when the sawmill settlement's population hovered around 200 citizens.

1 Herringshaw, Thos. W, *Local and National Poets of America*, American Publishers' Association; Chicago, IL; 1890, p.179
2 Robinson, Edgar Sutton, D.D., *The Presbyterian Ministerial Directory*, Vol. I; Oxford, Ohio, 1898, p. 416

The Methodists had placed MacMurray in charge of the Fayette and Manistique Circuit, which extended nearly 40 miles along the northern shore of Lake Michigan in the Upper Peninsula. MacMurray traversed this wild and largely uninhabited circuit nearly every Sabbath with very few exceptions.[3] While in Manistique, MacMurray stayed at the home of the Superintendent of the Chicago Lumbering Company, William Colwell and his family. Also staying at the home was Colwell's sister-in-law, Mary Barnes (the future Mrs. MacMurray) and the secretary of the lumber company, John Mersereau. [4]The children in the community, including Colwell's young sons Elmer and Fred, loved him.

Manistique's first school house where MacMurray held church services. Photo Courtesy Schoolcraft County Historical Society.

Church services took place in the little village school, located in the triangle park on present day Cedar Street. MacMurray was multi-talented with a flair for the dramatic. He could not only preach, but also sang and played the melodeon. His sermons were both entertaining and morally instructive. Often, he would act out a scene to drive home his message. In one sermon on the evils of intemperance, he portrayed a drunken

---

3   "A Crack in the Ice," *Madison Daily Democrat*, Madison, Wisconsin, Feb. 20, 1892, p.2; Reprinted from the *Detroit Free Press*.
4   August Klagstad, *Klagstad-Halverson Family History*, Minneapolis, Minnesota, August, 1946, pp.32, 39-40.

father coming home to abuse his family. Taking the kerosene lamp from the teacher's desk, he held it at arm's length as his body trembled with emotion.[5] The congregation could easily imagine what would happen next.

During December of 1876, MacMurray experienced a narrow escape while sledding across the ice of Garden Bay with his horse and cutter. He had been asked to officiate at a wedding in the home of a wealthy lumber dealer, and MacMurray did not want to be late. The shortcut across the ice would subtract nearly twelve miles from his journey. The young circuit rider had observed farmers crossing the bay with their teams and wagons just a few days before, and he presumed that the ice was safe.[6]

When nearly at the midpoint of his trip across the bay, MacMurray's horse suddenly stopped. The animal's acute hearing had detected the sound of barking dogs. As he scanned his surroundings, MacMurray understood what was matter. A pack of hungry wolves was emerging from the woods along the shore and would soon give chase. The clergyman applied the whip to his horse, and readied his revolver which he always carried with him on these treks. With the wolves gaining ground, the horse suddenly slowed as s six-inch crack in the ice appeared ahead. MacMurray turned the horse around, going back a short distance before taking another run at crossing the gap. It took three tries before the terrified animal braved the leap, momentarily breaking through the ice but reemerging so quickly that horse, cutter and passenger were unharmed. Meanwhile, the wolves had closed the distance and were surrounding the cutter, MacMurray took aim with his revolver and fired. The noise startled the pursuing pack enough that the pursuit of the wolves was slowed. This was repeated several times until the lumberman's house finally came into view. With the last chamber in his revolver emptied, the wolves broke off their chase. Fearful of civilization, the pack would have to satisfy their hunger elsewhere.[7]

Following the wedding, the lumberman handed MacMurray a check for five hundred dollars, perceiving correctly that the young minister "was not too overburdened with worldly goods." With his horse having been well rubbed down and blanketed, MacMurray returned safely to Manistique by another route.[8]

5   August Klagstad, *Klagstad-Halverson Family History*, p.32
6   "A Crack in the Ice," *Madison Daily Democrat*, Madison, Wisconsin, Feb. 20, 1892, p.2; Reprinted from the *Detroit Free Press*.
7   Ibid.
8   Ibid.

MacMurray was also an accomplished writer who published several volumes of poetry. His best known works included *The Legend of the Delaware Valley and Other Poems* and *After Hours*. His first book of poetry was entitled *In Danger and Out of It Again* and was published in 1877.[9]

> **THOS. J. MAC MURRAY ARRESTED.**
>
> Poet, Preacher and Newspaper Man, Formerly of Madison and Milwaukee.
>
> Word arrives from Manistique, Mich., of the arrest of Thomas J. MacMurray, editor of The Manistique News, on the charge of criminal libel on complaint of F. Riggs, prosecuting attorney of Schoolcraft county, and that he is now under $300 bail. Mr. MacMurray was formerly a resident of Wisconsin, and known to many Madisonians and Milwaukeeans, in both of which cities he spent some years. He is known to the literary world as the author of a book of poems, published at the office of The Madison Democrat in 1887. At that time he was attending the Wisconsin University Law school. Mr. MacMurray came to Milwaukee in the fall of 1887, and did some newspaper work. Later he was employed by several prominent mercantile firms as a writer of advertisements. He is a practical printer, and at one time was engaged in preaching in the Methodist sect. Mr. MacMurray is a writer of acknowledged ability, and is a cultivated man. His friends here will regret to learn that he has, in his editorial capacity, run against a libel suit.

Article from *The Weekly Sentinel*, Milwaukee, WI. August 13, 1891, p.1

In October of 1877, MacMurray married his sweetheart, Mary Barnes, in a ceremony at Manistique. When his new bride became pregnant with their first child in 1879, the family relocated to Oconto, Wisconsin. He was admitted to the Wisconsin Bar in 1883 and later attended the University of Wisconsin, graduating in 1885 with a law degree.

During the late 1880s MacMurray relocated again to Hamilton, Ohio where he found success on the lecture circuit. His popular presentations were filled with humor and sentiment. His travels took him to towns throughout Ohio, Indiana and Kentucky. He supplemented his income with published poems in the *Detroit Free Press, Daily Inter Ocean* and the *Milwaukee Sentinel*.

Changing course yet again, MacMurray returned to Manistique in April of 1890 to become publisher of the *Manistique News*. MacMurray almost immediately became embroiled in the battle to rid the county of corrupt saloon keepers who promoted prostitution and other forms of vice. When charges were not forthcoming against Seney saloon keeper Dan Dunn for the murder of Steve Harcourt in May of 1891, MacMurray accused the Prosecuting Attorney, William Riggs, of corruption. Riggs brought a libel suit against MacMurray, but the editor was acquitted after testifying on his own behalf. When news of the acquittal reached Bessemer, the editor of the

---

9   Edgar Sutton Robinson, D.D. p.416

Gogebic Iron Spirit concluded "MacMurray must have told the truth."[10] MacMurray continued as editor of the *Manistique News* until September of 1893 when his printing office was totally destroyed in Manistique's great fire.

MacMurray spent the remainder of his life as a Presbyterian clergyman, being licensed in September of 1894 and ordained in April of 1895. He was pastor at Gladstone, Michigan from 1895-97 and later served in numerous congregations throughout the Midwest. He ended his career in Seattle, Washington. MacMurray died on February 14, 1918 at age 65.[11] His famous grandson, Fred MacMurray was known to most children growing up in the 1960s as Stephen Douglas on the television series, "My Three Sons."

10 The Gogebic Iron Spirit, Bessemer, MI., November 17, 1891, p.1.
11 "To Hold Funeral of Pastor Monday" *Seattle Daily Times,* Feb. 16, 1918 p.7

Chapter Fifteen:
A Lightkeeper's Story

Manistique's longest serving light keeper, Walter Ottosen, was born at Washington Island, Wisconsin on July 18, 1876. He was the youngest of three surviving children born to Danish immigrants, Lars Peter Ottosen and Marie (Nielson) Ottosen. Walter's siblings included George, age eight, and four year old Morris. Walter never knew his mother who died when he was a small child in October of 1878.[1]

Walter Ottosen, circa 1920. Photo Courtesy Carol Dixson.

Lars Ottosen worked as a cooper, making barrels for fishermen to preserve their catch in salt brine.[2] Unable to both care for his young family and earn a living, Ottosen sailed to Rowley's Bay on the Door Peninsula. There he found Christine Pedersen and convinced her to return with him to Washington Island to care for his three young sons.[3] Christine and the boys bonded almost immediately, forming a loving and nurturing relationship. Lars and Christine were married less than a month later on July 4, 1879.[4]

1 Dick, Leora C. Sorensen, *The Ottosens (A Family History)* Updated, Revised, and Compiled by George L. Smith, January 18, 1992 p.11
2 Ibid. p. 11
3 Ibid, pp. 12-13
4 Ibid, p.13

When Walter was 12 years old, the family moved from the fishing village to a farm on Washington Island, where he spent the remainder of his boyhood years.[5] With the outbreak of the Spanish American War in April of 1898, Walter enlisted in the 3rd United States Infantry and went into training camp at Fort Snelling, Minnesota. Walter's unit sailed for Cuba from Mobile, Alabama on June 22, 1898. During the campaign in Cuba, Ottosen participated in the battles of El Caney, Santiago and San Juan Hill. With the end of the fighting, Ottosen was placed on sentry duty, guarding Spanish prisoners of war.[6]

The 3rd Infantry was returned to Fort Snelling at the close of the campaign in Cuba. Two weeks later, Ottosen and 85 men from his company were dispatched to Leech Lake, Minnesota, to put down an Indian uprising.[7] Chippewa tribal members believed that they were not receiving fair prices from the lumber companies for timber cut on reservation land. Other long-standing grievances simmered beneath the surface. The conflict boiled over into a violent skirmish on October 5, 1898. The company's losses included one officer and five enlisted men killed and ten others wounded. Casualties among the tribal members were undetermined, but at least one individual was killed.

Following the skirmish at Leech Lake, the 3rd Infantry was sent to the Philippines where the regiment participated in the battles of Malolos, San Isidro and Luzon. During this campaign, Ottosen was wounded in the right arm and also became ill with tropical fever. He was sent to a hospital in San Francisco with six months remaining on his three year enlistment. After he recovered, he served out his time in the army as a guard at Alcatraz military prison.[8]

While stationed at Fort Snelling, Walter met and fell in love with Althea Current. The couple was married on November 10, 1902 and started a family.[9]

5 Ibid.
6 "Keeper Of Manistique Lighthouse To Retire Oct. 1st, After 38 Years," Escanaba Daily Press, Escanaba, MI. Sept. 12, 1941, p12
7 Ibid.
8 Ibid.
9 Dick, Leora C. Sorensen, *The Ottosens (A Family History)* p. 52

Walter Ottosen (left) in his Spanish American War Uniform. Photo Courtesy Carol Dixson.

Ottosen entered the lighthouse service in 1903 at Manitowoc before going to Kenosha as assistant keeper. He also served as an assistant keeper at Rock Island and Menominee. He was promoted in 1912 and assigned as the light keeper at Pilot Island, a rocky, isolated outpost in Lake Michigan. Althea and the older children lived on nearby Washington Island so the children could attend school. Walter looked after the younger ones on Pilot Island. By 1920, the family had grown to include eight children.

The death of light keeper Charles Corlett in 1920 created the vacancy for Ottosen to transfer to Manistique as head light keeper. The Manistique lighthouse was built in 1916 and became operational on August 17, 1916.

It stood at the end of the east breakwater. A two-story duplex was built at the end of Range Street as a keepers' residence, 1200 feet from the inner end of the east breakwater.

Althea Ottosen had been growing increasingly dissatisfied in her marriage, leaving Walter and the children for the first time in 1925. Several more separations followed before the marriage finally ended in divorce on April 20, 1928. Walter was granted custody of the couple's four remaining minor children. Walter had been raising these children alone for the past three years, and once the divorce was finalized, he sought a new wife. Walter reportedly found his second wife, Roseline (Webb) Taylor, through either a newspaper or magazine ad. Walter drove to Canada to bring Rose and her daughter Kathleen back to Manistique. The couple was married in Manistique on September 7, 1929. The Ottosen children became very fond of Rose and their new step-sister Kathleen. Rose enjoyed cooking and baking for the children and entertaining her friends from church. Kathleen loved to play classical music on the piano.

Manistique Light House (1916), SCHS Photo.

Walter Ottosen spent a total of 38 years in the lighthouse service, retiring on October 1, 1941. He received the efficiency star for excellence in operating the lighthouse at Manistique for five consecutive years prior to his retirement. Ottosen and his wife Rose moved to Florida after his retirement. Rose passed away in 1949 and Walter died on March 27, 1960 at age 83.

The Lightkeeper's home is now a private residence.

Light keepers in Manistique included: Charles Corlett (1917-1920), Walter Ottosen (1920-1941), Walter Hansen (1941-1947), Thomas Brennan (1947), William Kellar (1947-1952), Anton Jessen Jr. (1952-1954) and Peter Scott (1954-1961).

First Assistant light keepers included: Thomas Nelson (1914-1917), William Renier (1917-1921), Raymond Buttars (1930-1941), Earl Malloch (1941-1942), Samuel Anderson (1947-1956) and William Schult (1956). Bert Walthers served as 2nd Assistant light keeper from 1934-1941. The light was fully automated in 1969.

Chapter Sixteen:
Alexander Richards and the Flat Iron Block

Alexander Richards was born on September 26, 1844 in Quebec, Canada to Lambert and Serafine (Serois) Richards, Alex was the eldest in a sibling group of eight children. Little is known about his early life in Canada. He immigrated to Michigan in 1866 at age 22 and resided at Fayette where he operated a butcher shop. Richards married Roxanna Knapp in Delta County on January 2, 1869. Seven children were born from this union.

Alexander Richards, Photo Courtesy Anthony Perkins Collection

The family lived in Garden, Michigan for a time, but moved to Manistique in 1876. While living in Manistique the family resided in a large home on the corner of Cedar and Walnut Street, which was the future site of the A. S. Putnam drug store.[1] Richard's daughter Ellen remembered eight people living in the home, including a servant. The servant was a necessity, as Richards' wife Roxanne went blind. Richards was reportedly very kind to all his children, and only repri-

1 Burns, Ellen Richards, *The Richards Family, News of 87 years Ago – Dating from September 15, 1873 to 1960*, Unpublished Manuscript; Germfask, Burns Michigan 1960

manded them when they moved items in the home which made it difficult for Roxanne to find things. He had a playhouse built for his daughters in the back yard complete with a toy cook stove.

During the late 1870's and early 80's Richards drove the stage daily from Manistique to Garden and delivered the mail. He also owned a livery stable on Pearl Street. Richards hired a black man, George Washington Bowers to manage the livery business.[2] Another venture was an ice cream store. Imagine owning an ice cream shop in the days before refrigeration and what a special treat that must have been in the pioneer village.

Richards was one of the few individuals who had title to property in the pioneer village. He did not share the prejudices of the owners of the Chicago Lumbering Company who owned nearly all the land in Manistique. The lumbermen were strong believers in temperance and sought to keep the town free of saloons. The deeds to all the property owned by the lumber company prohibited use of their land for the sale of alcohol, to wit:

> "It is understood and agreed between the respective parties hereto that all lands herein mentioned shall never be used by the party of the second part, its successors or assigns, for the business of manufacturing, storing or selling intoxicating liquors, whether distilled or fermented, nor for a house or place of prostitution or assignation, nor for any business or occupation prohibited or punished by the law of the land."

When Dan Heffron and his brother Dennis were seeking property on which to build a saloon, Alexander Richards obliged. The Heffron's Arcade Saloon soon stood at the busy intersection of Pearl and Water Streets ready to serve thirsty workers going to and from the Chicago Lumbering Company mill. With the sale of property to Heffron, all the lumber barons' efforts to keep Manistique a "dry" community were thwarted.

The Richards family lost three of their seven children while living in Manistique. A daughter Mary died in infancy in April of 1877. Twenty-one-month-old Anna died in March of 1881 and four-year-old Mary (the second child bearing that name) succumbed from small pox in June of 1882. One year later, in 1883, Alex Richards moved his family from their home on Cedar Street to a farm east of Manistique. His nine-year-old daughter Ellen remembered feeling sad about leaving the home where she had enjoyed so many happy times, but the move to the farm allowed

2 Ibid.

their father to spend much more time at home with his wife and children.³ Fear of losing more children to contagious diseases such as small pox and scarlet fever may also have been a factor.

A rare image of Pearl Street in the 1880's. Richard's ice cream shop is pictured on the left. Photo courtesy of Anthony Perkins.

Richards passed away on October 18, 1893 at the age of 49. The cause of his illness had baffled the doctors attending him. His funeral was one of the largest ever seen in Manistique with hundreds of citizens joining the procession to Lakeview Cemetery. The *Pioneer* reported that nearly every livery rig in the city had been pressed into service for the solemn procession.

Richard's daughter, Ellen (Richards) Burns wrote in 1960 that "regardless of the seeming faults of my dad, he did many kind deeds for children and for many who had trouble, but that he never allowed anyone he helped to talk about it. I have always been very proud of my father, Alex Richards, and God Bless him. I know he is resting in peace."⁴

3   Ibid.
4   Ibid.

Chapter Seventeen:
John Ira Bellaire, Merchant, Conservationist and Historian

Manistique booster, John Ira Bellaire was born in November of 1871. His family moved to White Pigeon in northern Lower Michigan when John was still a young child. There his parents, John and Agnes Bellaire purchased a small farm and struggled to support a growing family. John worked on the farm helping his father until he reached his eighteenth birthday, when he went out on his own.[1]

John Ira Bellaire, Photo courtesy Google Books

Bellaire took advantage of every opportunity he could to attend school. He worked at odd jobs on weekends, including splitting wood to earn money for books and tuition. During the summer he worked as a clerk in a grocery store. Once school started in the fall he continued working before and after school. He was finally able to graduate in June of 1891.[2]

In need of money to pay a grocery bill, Bellaire decided to try his hand at teaching. After passing the required exam, he obtained a teaching certificate, He taught for one year at a school near South Boardman, Michigan,

---

1 *Men of Progress: Embracing Biographical Sketches of Representative Michigan Men*; Evening News Association, Detroit, Michigan; 1900. P. 160.
2 Ibid.

in Kalkaska County. The school was one of the most challenging in the district. The superintendent had difficulty keeping a teacher for more than a few weeks, as the older boys physically threw their instructors out of the building or intimidated them to the point that they quit. After school started in the fall, Bellaire enjoyed a few peaceful weeks, as the bigger boys were still at home helping with the harvest. When the older boys returned to school, Bellaire discovered that most of them were taller and heavier than he. Nevertheless, things went along agreeably for a while, with the exception of some teasing of the younger boys. The ringleader was a young man named Johnson, who was the school bully. As the term went on, the older boys became more contemptuous. Bellaire was sure that he and young Johnson would clash, and that either he would become a bruised and battered ex-teacher, or that he would have one or two fewer students.[3]

The matter was settled right after the Christmas holiday. While climbing the stairs with an armful of wood, Bellaire was accosted by Johnson and another of the larger boys. He managed to drop the wood before being knocked backward in the snow with Johnson on top of him. The shock of the incident must have scared the other boy who ran off. Struggling to defend himself, the young teacher grabbed the boy's throat and began to choke him. When he let up, he washed the boys face with snow. This action was repeated several times until Johnson was finally vanquished. With the entire class watching, Johnson started to cry thus ending his days as the school bully. The boy's attitude was transformed after the incident, and he became one of Bellaire's best students.[4]

Bellaire had one more trial to pass through when the next day brought Mrs. Johnson to his classroom. She was a large woman and Bellaire was careful to keep his desk between himself and his accuser. She vented for nearly an hour over the mistreatment of her innocent son. It was only then that Bellaire was able to calmly explain what happened leaving her "somewhat pacified."[5]

In the spring of 1893, Bellaire answered a "help wanted" ad for a clerk's position in a general store at Seney, Michigan, with a salary of 35 dollars per month. In 1895 he was promoted to general manager. On September 24, 1896, Bellaire married Sarah Boynton, who was to be his devoted

[3] John Bellaire Recalls Old Schoolmaster Days in Lower Part of State; *Escanaba Daily Press*, Saturday, September 19, 1931, p.11
[4] Ibid.
[5] Ibid.

companion for over 60 years. One year later Bellaire was appointed Postmaster at Seney and by 1899 he had saved enough money to buy the store.[6]

A keen observer of others, Bellaire came to know the people of Seney including the lumberjacks, the saloon keepers and the ordinary citizens and farmers who came to the store to buy their groceries and pick up their mail. The town, which was to become infamous for sin and mayhem, was Bellaire's home for over a decade during its heyday as a booming lumbering settlement.

With the end of the big pine era, Bellaire relocated to Manistique where he opened a five and dime variety store. His first store opened for business in 1927. Offering quality merchandise, affordable prices, and friendly, courteous service; his enterprise thrived. By 1938 he was able to open a second store on the west side of Manistique.

A primitive raft on the Big Spring, circa 1880's. Photo Courtesy Schoolcraft County Historical Society, Fox Family Collection

It was in the early 1920's that Bellaire became a devoted fan of the Big Spring. At that time the area was remote and undeveloped. Surrounded by fallen timber and debris left over from the lumber companies, Bellaire immediately recognized the unique beauty of the spring and the need to preserve it for future generations. Though Bellaire could easily have purchased the property, he felt it could only be protected through public

---

6 *Men of Progress: Embracing Biographical Sketches of Representative Michigan Men*; Evening News Association, Detroit, Michigan; 1900. P. 160.

ownership. In 1926, in cooperation with Frank Book, who was a partner in the Palms Book Land Company of Detroit, Bellaire arranged for the sale of 90 acres of land including the spring to the State of Michigan for $10.00. The land was to be forever designated as a state park bearing the name, Palms Book State Park.

Besides promoting the Big Spring as a major tourist attraction, Bellaire spent his later years documenting the area's history, writing a series of articles for the *Escanaba Daily Press* about the history of Seney in the wild days of the big pine era.

Chapter Eighteen:
The McCanna Brothers – Pioneer Lawmen

The early history of law enforcement in Schoolcraft County is closely tied to the McCanna family. The family patriarch, Henry McCanna was born in 1822 in county Donegal, Ireland. McCanna immigrated first to Canada before settling in the Vermont/New York area in the mid 1840s. Henry married Nancy (Anna) O'Kane in 1845 in Sandy Hill, New York. Ten children were born to this union, eight of whom survived into adulthood.

John McCanna, Photo courtesy Susan Cucchiarella.

Pioneer Schoolcraft County Sheriff John McCanna, was born on April 27, 1847 in Swanton, Vermont. The family moved to Glen Falls, New York in 1850 and then on to Painted Post, New York where He was employed in the lumber industry.[1]

With the outbreak of the American Civil War in April of 1961, Henry McCanna volunteered with the 23rd New York Infantry in May of 1861. Henry's son John McCanna, age 14, had his own plans for service, coming to Washington D.C., intending to join the 107th New York regiment as a drum major. These plans came to naught after a visit with his father in a Washington army camp. Young McCanna was ordered home by his father to help care for his mother and five younger siblings including Henry Jr., Charles, Alexander, William and Mary.[2]

---

1 McCanna genealogical information provided by Susan Cucchiarella.
2 John McCanna Obituary, *Manistique PioneerTribune*, reprinted from the *Ontonagon Herald*, August 1930

In September of 1864, 17 year old John McCanna added a year to his age and enlisted in the 107th New York Infantry, joining his father who had reenlisted into the same regiment in January of 1864. Father and son shared a tent, serving in General William T. Sherman's army during the famous march from Atlanta to the sea. With the close of the war, father and son returned home to Painted Post, New York. John McCanna moved west to Harrisville, Michigan, in 1867 where he remained for 12 years. He married Anna Hogue on October 21, 1869.[3]

John's parents, Henry and Nancy McCanna, moved to the lumbering settlement of Manistique in 1878, and were joined a year later by John McCanna and his family. John and his father were both employed in the lumber industry—John working as a saw filer in the mill. Other members of the McCanna family who resided for a time in Manistique included Charles, Henry, William, Alexander, Mary, Elizabeth and George.

With the total destruction of the town of Onota (in present day Alger County) by fire in 1879, the county seat of Schoolcraft County was moved to Manistique. John Costello was the first person to hold the office of Sheriff in the new county seat of Manistique, serving from 1879 through 1881.

John McCanna was elected as Schoolcraft County Sheriff with his term beginning in 1882. The county's first jail was a one-story wooden structure, 25 feet by 45 feet. It was heated by a wood furnace with ventilating flues in each cell. There were five cells made from wood plank, with a separate room to accommodate a bath tub and privy. This jail was totally destroyed by fire on January 25, 1884. Without a building to incarcerate prisoners, Sheriff McCanna was required to transport offenders to St. Ignace until a new jail could be erected.

In the fall of 1884 voters approved the construction of a new jail which opened in 1885. The new lockup was a two-story structure measuring 18 feet by 24 feet. There were six jail cells on the first floor. The 6 foot square cells were constructed with iron bars and were heated in the winter by a wood stove in the corridor. Toilet facilities consisted of a bucket in each cell. Five small rooms on the second story housed female prisoners and boys. These were also used for the mentally ill while awaiting transport to the Northern Michigan Asylum in Traverse City. This jail served the citizens of Schoolcraft County until 1958 when it was replaced by our current jail building.

3   Ibid.

Henry McCanna, Photo Courtesy Susan Cucchiarella.

John McCanna was followed in the sheriff's office by his brother Henry beginning in 1886. Their younger brother, William McCanna, held the office of Under Sheriff. Dennis Heffron ended the McCanna's hold on the sheriff's office, winning election in 1888

With his term of office over, John McCanna returned to work in the lumber industry. He remained in Manistique until 1897 before moving with his family to Green Bay, Wisconsin. In 1904 McCanna moved to Ontonagon, Michigan where he remained until his death in August of 1930 at age 83.

Henry McCanna Jr. remained in Manistique through at least 1930 when he was 81 years old. He died in San Diego, California in April of 1936 at age 87.

A circa 1885 photo of the new Schoolcraft County Jail and sheriff's residence. A portion of the original courthouse built in 1883 can be seen on the far right. Photo Courtesy SCHS.

Bibliography

Articles:

Byers, David C. with the assistance of Willis Dunbar, "Utopia in Upper Michigan," *The Quarterly Review of the Michigan Alumnus*, Winter 1957

Ronning, N. N. "August Klagstad, Artist" *The Friend,* March, 1938

Books:

Anderson, Olive M. *Utopia in Upper Michigan*, Northern Michigan University Press, Marquette, Michigan, 1982

Beeson, Harvey Child, *Beeson's Marine Directory of the Northwestern Lake*s, Eleventh Edition, Chicago, Ill., 1898, Page 194

Carter, James L. *Superior, A State For The North Country,* The Pilot Press, Marquette, MI. 1980

Crowe, William S. *Lumberjack: Inside An Era in the Upper Peninsula of Michigan,* 3[d] ed. Skandia, Mich. North Country Publishing, 2002

Dick, Leora C. Sorensen, *The Ottosens (A Family History)* Updated, Revised, and Compiled by George L. Smith, January 18, 1992

Dodge, Roy L. *Michigan Ghost Towns, Volume III Upper Peninsula* Tawas City, Mich.: Glendon Publishing, 1973

Garden Peninsula Historical Society, *Our Heritage,* 1982

Hayes, Arthur Garfield *Let Freedom Ring,* New York: Livenright Publishing Corp. 1937

Hennepin, Louis, *Discovery of Louisiana,* Translated from the Edition of 1683, by John Gilmay Shea, New York, 1880

Herringshaw, Thos. W, *Local and National Poets of America*, American Publishers' Association; Chicago, IL; 1890

Howard, Robertson, Editor, *The Northwestern Reporter*, Volume 19, May 8-July 5, 1884, Saint Paul: West Publishing Company 1884

Kleppner, Paul, *The Cross of Culture: A Social Analysis of Midwestern Politics 1850-1900*, New York, The Free Press, Div. of MacMillan Co., 1970

Lloyd's Register of Shipping 1831, London, England, 1831

Men of Progress: Embracing Biographical Sketches of Representative Michigan Men; Evening News Association, Detroit, Michigan; 1900.

Neuschel, Fred, *Lives & Legends of the Christmas Tree Ships,* Ann Arbor: The University of Michigan Press, 2007

Orr, Jack, *Lumberjacks and River Pearls* Manistique, Mich.: Pioneer Tribune, Dec. 1979

Parkman, Francis, *LaSalle and the Discovery of the Great West, Vol. I,* Boston: Little Brown and Co., New York: J. F. Taylor and Co. 1897

Pennington, Rochelle, *The Historic Christmas Tree Ship* Pathways Press, 2004;

Quick, Arthur C. *A Genealogy of the Quick Family In America (1625-1942),* Privately Published by Arther C. Quick, South Haven and Palisades Park, Mich., 1942

Robinson, Edgar Sutton, D.D., *The Presbyterian Ministerial Directory,* Vol. I; Oxford, Ohio, 1898

Skinner, Emory Fiske, *Reminiscences,* Vestal Printing Co., Chicago, Illinois 1908

Government Publications:

Michigan Reports. Report of Cases Heard and Decided in The Supreme Court of Michigan from January 4 to October 13, 1860. Thomas M. Cooley, Reporter. Vol. IV. Being Volume VIII of the Series. Ann Arbor: Published by the Reporter. Detroit: F. Raymond & Co. and S. D. Elwood. 1860

Report of the Attorney General of the State of Michigan for the Year Ending June 30, A.D. 1892, Adolphus A. Ellis, Attorney General, Lansing, Robert Smith & Co., State Printers and Binders, 1892

Report of the Attorney General of the State of Michigan for the Year Ending June 30, A.D. 1893, Adolphus A. Ellis, Attorney General, Lansing, Robert Smith & Co., State Printers and Binders, 1893

United States Congressional Serial Set, 58th Congress, 2nd Session

Manuscripts:

Bellaire, John I. *Hiawatha Colony: Its Rise and Fall,* Bellaire Papers, Schoolcraft County Historical Society archives

Burns, Ellen Richards, *The Richards Family, News of 87 years Ago – Dating from September 15, 1873 to 1960,* Unpublished Manuscript; Germfask, Burns Michigan 1960.

Byers, David C. *Abraham Sneathen Byers and the Hiawatha Village Association,* July 1,1955, Schoolcraft County Historical Society archives

Kemp, Jane *August Klagstad Biography*, Luther College, Decorah, Iowa; July, 2004

Killelea, Elaine *History of First Lutheran,* First Lutheran Church, Portland, Maine, August, 1999

Klagstad, August *Klagstad-Halvorsen Family History* (Minneapolis, Minnesota, January 1946)

Saunders, Harvey C. *Harvey C. Saunders Papers,* Michigan State University Archives and Historical Collections, East Lansing, Michigan

Newspapers:

Associated Press
Buffalo Courier
Cambridge City Tribune
Chicago Daily Inter-Ocean
Chicago Daily News
Chicago Record-Herald
Chicago Tribune
Daily Inter-Ocean
Democratic Union
Duluth News Tribune
Escanaba Daily Press
Evening News
Headline News
Ironwood Advocate
Ironwood Daily Globe
Kokomo Dispatch
Kokomo Saturday Tribune
Gogebic Iron Spirit
Goshen Democrat
Grand Traverse Herald
Herald Press
Madison Daily Democrat
Manistique Courier
Manistique Pioneer Tribune
Manitoulin West Recorder
Manitowoc Herald-Times

Milwaukee Journal
Milwaukee Sentinel
News Palladium
Omaha World Herald
Oshkosh Daily Northwestern
Saturday Morning Star
Sault Ste. Marie News
Schoolcraft County Pioneer
Seattle Daily Times
Semi-Weekly Pioneer
Sentinel
Sheboygan Press
Sheboygan Press-Telegram
Sturgeon Bay Advocate
Sunday Sentinel
Sunday Sun
Tri-Weekly Pioneer,
Waterloo Courier
Weekly Tribune

Government Archives

Library of Michigan, Lansing, MI., Microfilm records of the George F. Fuller Post, Grand Army of the Republic

Manistee County Probate Court Archives, Estate of Daniel D. Ruggles

National Archives, Civil War Pension File, Constant M. Ruggles

National Archives, Civil War Widow's Pension File for Elizabeth A. Reynard, beneficiary of Solomon A. Reynard, 57th Indiana Infantry, Co. E

National Archives, Seymour T. Montgomery Civil War Pension Index, Application number 643764

Schoolcraft County Circuit Court Archives, Case No. 116, People v Daniel and Dennis Heffron

Schoolcraft County Circuit Court Archives, Case No. 112, People v. Dennis, Larry and Dan Heffron

Schoolcraft County Circuit Court Archives, Case No. 320, People v. Daniel Heffron, Circuit Court Journal No. 1

Schoolcraft County Circuit Court Archives, People v. Walter Thomas Mills

Schoolcraft County Circuit Court Archives, Margaret E. Stark v. John Stark

Schoolcraft County Circuit Court Archives, Maud Ruggles Robbins vs. Eugene Robbins

Schoolcraft County Probate Court Archives, Estate of Wright E. Clarke

Schoolcraft County Probate Court Archives, In the Matter of Will F. Montgomery

Miscellaneous:

Kokomo Indiana Public Library, Kokomo, Indiana, Sipe Family Bible

Valparaiso University Archives, Indiana State Normal School 1885 Course Catalog

NAACP, *Closing argument of Clarence Darrow in People v. Henry Sweet in the Recorders Court, Detroit, Michigan, May 11, 1926.* Transcript published by the National Association for the Advancement of Colored People.

www.ingramcontent.com/pod-product-compliance
Lightning Source LLC
Chambersburg PA
CBHW070810100426
42742CB00012B/2320